Rejoice Always

REJOICE *Always*

Cultivating Joy with Six Saintly Companions

Sheri Wohlfert

Our Sunday Visitor
Huntington, Indiana

Nihil Obstat
Msgr. Michael Heintz, Ph.D.
Censor Librorum

Imprimatur
✠ Kevin C. Rhoades
Bishop of Fort Wayne-South Bend
October 30, 2024

The *Nihil Obstat* and *Imprimatur* are official declarations that a book is free from doctrinal or moral error. It is not implied that those who have granted the Nihil Obstat and Imprimatur agree with the contents, opinions, or statements expressed.

30 29 28 27 26 25 2 3 4 5 6 7 8 9

Our Sunday Visitor Publishing Division
Our Sunday Visitor, Inc.
200 Noll Plaza
Huntington, IN 46750
www.osv.com
1-800-348-2440

ISBN: 978-1-63966-260-9 (Inventory No. T2930)
1. RELIGION—Christianity—Saints & Sainthood.
2. RELIGION—Christian Living—Spiritual Growth.
3. RELIGION—Christianity—Catholic.

eISBN: 978-1-63966-261-6
LCCN: 2024949919

Cover design: Amanda Falk
Cover art: AdobeStock
Interior design: Amanda Falk

PRINTED IN THE UNITED STATES OF AMERICA

Contents

Introduction

These things I have spoken to you, that my joy may be in you, and that your joy may be full. — John 15:11

As I strolled through a farmers' market on a sunny Saturday morning, I came across a vegetable I knew nothing about. I had no earthly notion how to prepare it or even what it tasted like, but I bought one of the darn things because it was a deep purple — which is one of my favorite colors — and because it was a vegetable, so I figured it had to be good for me. I took the eggplant home and stared at it, sitting on my counter, for days. The longer I kept it, the more puzzling it became. Eventually, it spoiled, and I tossed it out. To this day I still know nothing about the taste and preparation of an eggplant, but that silly vegetable taught me a lesson: There are plenty of good things we can add to our life, but if we don't know how to use them, appreciate them, absorb them, and nurture them, we miss out on their value.

We were created out of love in the image and likeness of God. He knit us in our mother's womb, and at the moment of our conception, his plan was crystal clear: for us to become saints and enjoy the rewards of eternal life in heaven with him. That truth should knock our socks off and fill our souls with joy, peace, and hope, strong enough to conquer all the wonkiness of our days. But more days than not, we forget the power of that truth. We think we have to muster up our own strength and holiness, slog our way through temptations and disappointments and struggles, and somehow put our wilted, soggy heads on the pillow at night hoping we did enough to edge our way a teeny-tiny bit closer to heaven.

The truth is that we were created to need God, to want him, and to be loved by him. As great as that seems, living as though we know it can seem as puzzling as that eggplant from the farmers' market. We need some information, some direction, some guidance, and some assurance — so, my friends, that is precisely what has spilled out onto the pages of this book! In his infinite love for us, God gives us the gifts and graces required to grow in holiness and become the saints we were created to be.

One of my favorite questions is "What is God doing in your life?" My answer to that question is — everything! I will be the first to admit, however, that that wouldn't have always been my answer. I spent decades thinking God's love had to be earned by completing a checklist of tasks. I was under the ridiculous notion that getting to heaven was my work and that it was evaluated as homework handed in at the end of the day. It wasn't until I let out a loud cry to the Lord, asking him to show me who he made me to be, that I understood the power of his grace, the depth of his love, and the stunning beauty of his joy. That's when my life changed. His grace is unending, his love is unrivaled, and his joy transforms every corner of our lives.

Joy is different than happiness. Happiness is what so many people seek, but it's fleeting, and it hinges on circumstances, events, or people that aren't created to last. Happiness is a glorious emotion, but it's made to come and go in bursts. True joy, though, comes from being firmly rooted in the will of God. It's that feeling of knowing you are exactly where you're supposed to be, doing exactly what you're supposed to be doing, and the Father who led you there is right there too. He is guiding, loving, instructing, and protecting you. He brings knowledge, wisdom, and peace to even the craziest, happiest, trickiest, scariest, most puzzling situations we can imagine. Being firmly rooted in the joy of the Lord means every situation and circumstance can be used for his glory and our sainthood ... even the ones we don't like or don't understand. Being rooted in the joy of the Lord makes us complete and completely his.

Joy is something we choose, over and over again. Joy opens our eyes to the ways the Lord is working in us and through us. Joy allows us to feel his peace, endure suffering, grow in humility and holiness, and live for his glory, not our own. Joy is the way we make sense out of the senseless and quiet the chaos of the world so that we can hear the voice of the creator.

If all this seems as unfamiliar and puzzling as that eggplant from the farmers' market seemed, then please read on and learn how to choose, embrace, and infuse joy into your life. As we journey toward days lived in the joy of the Lord, we will take our cue from three sources.

The first place we will draw wisdom and insight from is Sacred Scripture. One little nugget at a time, we will steep our minds and hearts in the guiding words of our Father. Second, we will befriend six saintly companions. In a world of influencers and social media show-and-tell, we don't always get the dose of "real and true" that our souls crave. We all need a solid example to follow, and it's helpful if the example is relatable, achievable, and authentic. The six saints we will walk with are exactly those things. I chose them because they represent the struggles and celebrations that touch each of our lives. They weren't perfect, but they woke up each morning with a burning desire to joyfully love the Lord a little harder than they had the day before.

Each one of us is like a novel written lovingly by our creator. Throughout the stories that are our lives, there will be triumph, tragedy, plot twists, and character changes. There will be chapters full of beauty and others that are startling and dramatic — but only the author of our lives knows what the next chapter holds. The fact that each of our lives has been perfectly crafted means that God is intimately and precisely intertwined in every part of our stories. When we look, we can see the fancy and amazing ways he is working constantly in the moments and events of our days. These ways tell captivating, lovely, and hopeful stories of his enormous passion for us, so the pages that lie ahead contain a collection of personal stories that shine a vivid light on the ways the Father shows up every day to be fancy and loving and merciful to his beloved sons and daughters.

In the letter of Saint James, we read that all good and perfect gifts are from above. We sometimes forget that we might view "good and perfect" through a different lens than the Father does. Sometimes the tough things in life turn out to be his greatest gifts. Living joyfully means we know God is involved in every little speck of our days and that he can use all things to help us grow in holiness. Each section of this book focuses on a gift from the Father designed to help us do exactly that, and in order to show us how to joyfully embrace each, we will walk with a saint who demonstrated how to live it out.

Heaven is a place of unfathomable joy. The Scriptures, saints, and stories shared here are intended to prepare us for that. Jesus didn't describe heaven as a mystical place — he described it as home. Welcome to the journey of becoming rooted in the joy of the Lord, on your way to sainthood and life in our true home.

The First Gift
Joyful Love

1
St. Marianne Cope

I do not expect a high place in heaven. I will be very grateful to have a little corner where I can love God for all eternity. — St. Marianne Cope

When I was a little girl and had a big job to do, my mom would always tell me the first step was to simply pick a starting spot. Little Sheri understood the big thing was to just get started. As I grew, logic and organization developed, and eventually that understanding blossomed into the art of beginning a task with the most important part. If we think about the task of joyfully growing in holiness, discovering the most important part is as simple as returning to the Gospel message. Again and again, Jesus taught that the most important thing is to love God and to love our neighbor. We experience contagious joy when we are doing the will of God, and the perfect spot to start cooperating with his perfect plan is to focus on love — the most important part. So, as we set out on this journey, we begin with the gift our souls were created to receive and share: the gift of love.

Godly love is so much more than a notion of happy, warm, fuzzy, comfortable feelings. As humans, we truly have a need to belong and a desire to feel valued. We spend our days seeking both from the world, but Scripture teaches that the true love we need comes from the Father. His love is the only true, worthy, dependable kind of love. And when we receive the Father's love, we are invited to share it with others. The Gospels call us to love when it's hard, to love the unlovable, and to offer love lavishly and consistently to all his children, especially when we won't be loved in return.

St. Marianne Cope was a living witness to exactly the kind of love Jesus taught.

Saint Marianne's deepest longing was to become a religious sister. But when her father became too sick to work, instead of entering the convent, she took up work in a textile factory to support her family. In God's timing, she became a sister of St. Francis of Assisi and set about the work of loving and serving the poor, sick, and outcast in central New York. Her greatest act of love for God's children came at the request of the government in Hawaii for sisters to serve those suffering with leprosy. Because of the enormous personal risk of contracting the disease, this request had been denied by many other religious orders, but Saint Marianne replied with an enthusiastic yes. With deep and abiding love and peace in her heart, she replied to the request with these words: "I am hungry for the work and I wish with all my heart to be one of the chosen ones, whose privilege it will be to sacrifice themselves for the salvation of the souls of the poor Islanders. … I am not afraid of any disease; hence, it would be my greatest delight even to minister to the abandoned 'lepers.'"

Saint Marianne and her sisters lovingly helped those with this dreaded, fatal disease to live with dignity. She built schools and clinics and worked tirelessly teaching them, praying with them, and having fun with them. With great compassion, she made sure they were taken care of physically, emotionally, and spiritually. She spent three and a half decades on the island of Molokai and died of natural causes, having never contracted the disease.

Saint Marianne, we pray for your intercession as we learn to accept and offer the radical gift of the Father's love.

St. Marianne Cope, pray for us!

2
Love Requires Sacrifice … Always

And walk in love, as Christ loved us and gave himself up for us, a fragrant offering and sacrifice to God. — Ephesians 5:2

Love requires sacrifice … always! What a powerful truth I seem to forget. Sacrifice often takes a back seat to convenience and comfort. We prefer easy, speedy, and painless and then wonder why we don't feel fulfilled. The important stuff, the stuff that leaves us joyful and alive — that's the stuff that involves love and requires sacrifice.

We are called by the greatest commandment to love, and the truth is that we can't follow that commandment without sacrifice. Sometimes that sacrifice is small — for instance, I loved my students during my years of teaching, but spending time in the evenings and on weekends to grade papers or plan lessons was a sacrifice. Other times the sacrifice is much bigger. I hugged a good friend at her father's wake recently; she lovingly told me she was so happy for her dad and that she found peace just thinking about him rejoicing and being free from pain. Her perspective and strength were inspiring, but the sacrifice of her love for her dad will weigh heavily on her days for quite a while.

Sometimes sacrifice needs to look like patience. Sometimes it needs to sound like a swallowed opinion. Sometimes it needs to appear as sand slipping through our fingers as we let go of the past or our own agenda. Sacrifice is loving people exactly how they are and where they are. Sometimes we're called to love someone just by being present, and there is sacrifice in keeping quiet and not trying to fix or change them.

The people who love us back make it easy to love, but we're also called to show Christ's love to those who can give nothing in return. Saint Marianne would say to the sisters who cared for the lepers whom society had abandoned that "I do not think of reward. I am working for God and do so cheerfully." Marianne loved and cared with her whole heart in a place few knew anything about, and she considered all the sacrifices that came with her work to be her joyful duty.

I think about all the times I've tried to find the perfect gift to show my love for someone. When I heard the line "Love requires sacrifice ... always" spoken by a movie character, I realized I'd been shopping the wrong way. The more we love, the more we should be willing to sacrifice. I love my children, but I'm not sure they always saw my carpool complaining as a loving sacrifice. "Love requires sacrifice ... always" can show up in doing the laundry and helping with homework and holding the flashlight in the rain so that Dave can figure out why the tractor is making a weird noise. This kind of love happens in the middle of the night after a kid has had a bad dream, or at the end of the day when you want to tune out the world, but someone you love just really wants to spill his heart.

There have been times when I've wondered if all the sacrifice of a relationship was worth it or if love was really supposed to be so hard and one-sided, but as I prayed with these words, I realized I was looking at it out of balance. Love and sacrifice aren't always equal. Sometimes we receive love far greater than we sacrifice, and sometimes the sacrifice is overwhelmingly greater than the love we receive.

We're able to sacrifice for and love others, but at some point, we expect to receive love in return. We want to feel there is something in it for us. But our call to love others isn't for us to get something in return. Love is so much bigger than all the warm, fuzzy feelings. Love is the duty of a disciple, and we do it best when we remember that each person who crosses our path is there so that we can show her the love of Christ. It's not about loving so that we can get something back; it's about loving so that we can love Jesus himself. When I look at Jesus on the cross, I find the truth — there is more love poured out on me than I could ever imagine. We may never be called to love with a sacrifice anywhere near that magnitude, but recalling his sacrifice for us helps put our teeny, little sacrifices for others in perspective.

To grow in joyful love: Who are you being asked to love today?

St. Marianne Cope, pray for us!

3
Living His Love

Be still, and know that I am God. — Psalm 46:10

I love to read articles and watch videos that make me laugh, make me think, and help me grow in discipleship. Social media highlights people who are "it." Influencers point us to products and habits and attitudes to help us be the envy of all, but more often than not, their messages are in direct opposition to our pursuit of sainthood. Instead of trying to be "it," perhaps we should focus on being God's. The holy men and women we call saints have better stories than anyone who might pop up in our newsfeed, and these folks are the supreme influencers. Not long ago I came across two very holy, humble women who seemed to have a message I needed to hear. St. Faustina Kowalska and St. Catherine of Siena were pretty big-deal women. Their lives were filled with devotion, service, humility, courage, and obedience. The way they loved and served the Lord and his people was simply astounding.

I was thinking about how much God must have loved these ladies, and I wondered what I should to do to make him love me more. I began to make a list in my head of all the things I needed to change and all the places I paled in comparison. I decided they must be in a completely separate category, one where they were doted on and revered by those on earth and in heaven. I mean, that would only make sense, since both Saint Faustina and Saint Catherine had visions and messages from God and his Son. They saw, they heard, and they physically felt his presence, so surely he loved them dearly.

It's true, he absolutely did, but he loved them in the same way he loves you and me. Their response to his love is where the huge difference lies. They drew closer and closer to him no matter the cost. No matter what craziness was going on in the world around them, he was absolutely the only thing they thought about, focused on, and lived for.

Despite their complete devotion to him, they were not always shielded from the hurts of the world. I was so surprised to learn that despite her amazing faith and interactions with Jesus, Faustina's superiors wrote in her file three sharp words: "No one special." Wow, can you imagine a woman as incredible as Saint Faustina being described that way? I think I would have been tempted to say,:"Hey, sister, how many times has Jesus appeared in your room to chat? No one special, my foot!" Saint Catherine was humbled as well. God spoke to her and said, "I am who am; you are she who is not." Talk about a truth that cuts you to the quick. Bam! I am; you aren't! I know she knew this absolute truth, but it would have been nice to lead with "I am God, and you are my beautiful daughter who serves with your whole self!" Judging by my reaction to these humbling zingers, it's pretty clear why Faustina and Catherine are the saints, and I am not.

Their stories contained a little lesson for me to get over myself. I tend to see things through the lens of "Look what I'm doing for you, God!" These ladies devoted their complete existence to him — I bought extra groceries for the food bank, prayed a few more Rosaries, and volunteered to lead morning prayer a couple times a week, and I think that makes me seem sparkly to

God. Saint Marianne spoke piercing truth when she said: "I do not expect a high place in heaven. I will be very grateful to have a little corner where I can love God for all eternity." Sheesh, I've got work to do!

The stories of the saints remind me that it's not my doing that makes the Father love me; it's my being. We are called to serve and pray, but mostly we're called to just be: Be his, be still, be humble, and be as close to him as we possibly can. Every experience that humbles us or stretches us or causes us to struggle is a moment to turn to him and be loved by him. He doesn't need me to put on a show to earn his love. He just needs me to show up and let him love me, through the struggles, disappointments, uncertainty, and all the humbling events that allow me to become small enough to find refuge in the shadow of his greatness and enormous love.

To grow in joyful love: Read a little about a saint or two and ask the Father how he might be using their examples to help you grow in faith.

St. Marianne Cope, pray for us!

4
Let Love Be the Reason

Whatever your task, work heartily, as serving the Lord and not men. — Colossians 3:23

One year I had two little boys in my class who were cousins. The two boys were good friends who laughed and played with everyone. One day we were playing sight word bingo, and one of the boys won a new pencil from the treasure box. A few games later, his cousin was still without a win, and he was lucky enough to win a second pencil. He returned to the table and, without saying a word, pushed the pencil across the table to his cousin. His eyes gave a silent thank you, and we all continued playing. Later that day, I mentioned to the generous cousin that I thought his actions had been very loving and kind. He just looked down at his shuffling feet and said, "I can only write with one pencil at a time, and besides, Jesus would have given his extra pencil to his cousin, I think." There just wasn't anything more to say, so I winked and told him I thought he made Jesus smile. I was touched because it wasn't about a new pencil at all; it was about a love sincere enough to recognize and comfort a simple disappointment.

God is waiting for our yes in teeny places as well as grand

ones. Out of fifty religious leaders asked to serve the lepers in Hawaii, Saint Marianne was the only one who said yes. She did it with complete confidence, joy, and delight, simply because she saw the need and the opportunity to love. Her work might have been much bigger than giving a pencil to a sad cousin, but the motivation was the same.

We worry a lot about what we should do, say, wear, and buy. Many of our decisions, even the simple ones, are balanced against some invisible social scale. What will others think if I do that or if my kids do this or if I show up wearing those? Every now and again, life has a way of wrinkling up the rug and tripping us. One weekend as I was doing some grocery shopping, I saw the Salvation Army bellringers. I thought, man, it's only November 24, and they are already posted outside every doorway of every store. I am always overcome with guilt if I pass by one without putting in some change. I guess I don't want others to think I'm stingy. I was completely ashamed of my attitude when I walked into the store.

As I trudged through the produce section, I thought of those volunteers who braved the cold and wind and snow to help those in need, and I was embarrassed that I was small enough to grumble about it. I remembered the story of the widow and her coins and realized I needed to think about things differently. She gave not from her surplus but from the only three coins she had, all for the love of God. As I was thinking about that, three small children took the pennies they were saving to go on the store pony ride and decided to put them in the Salvation Army bucket instead. The bell ringer thanked them and said in a loud cheerful voice, "May God bless you!" Those were the perfect words. They were the reminder I needed because those four words contained the whole meaning of "doing and giving out of love." The three little kids smiled and skipped all the way to their minivan.

The whole situation caused me to think about this verse

from Colossians in a new way. I'm not supposed to do things so that someone will notice or not notice me. I'm supposed to be generous with my time, talents, and resources because I want to love and serve the Lord, not man. Those little kids who turned over their pony ride pennies weren't excited because other shoppers had seen what they did; they were happy because they had done a loving, Christ-like thing.

As I drove home, I wondered what life would be like if I based all my actions on one simple question: How much can I love and please God today? What if I worried half as much about what he thought as about what my neighbor thought? And just to show off, God reminded me of this verse using the one thing guaranteed to get my attention: children! The cousins and the three kids with pennies — he used them to show me where I need to work.

To grow in joyful love: Prayerfully ask God to show you what small thing (or large thing) you can do to love and serve him today.

St. Marianne Cope, pray for us!

5
Circle of Love

O give thanks to the LORD, for he is good,
for his mercy endures for ever. — *Psalm 136:1*

On our way back to the classroom after Mass on Friday, one of my little first-grade lovelies looked up at me and said, "Mrs. Wohlfert, I know why God made the earth round." I asked him, "Why did God do that?" His reply was wise and priceless. He said: "Because round is a circle and a circle doesn't have a beginning or an end, and neither does God's love. It just keeps going and going and going and never stops. Wasn't that a good idea God had?" "One of his best," I answered with a wink and a smile.

We are so loved, aren't we! We have a God and Father who will love us forever and ever no matter what. He loves us with a love that will never end and never change. Even when we drift away, or forget to thank and praise him for all he does, he's still there, lovin' and lovin' and lovin'! I can't think of a single thing as dependable as that. But I think we get busy sometimes and forget what an awesome gift that is. Even greater is the fact that it comes to us freely. We don't have to earn it or deserve it or ask for it; God's love just there waiting for us to acknowledge and share it with others.

That Friday afternoon, I was cleaning up the classroom table, where the kids had been busy gluing a project made of spiral pasta and Popsicle™ sticks. The glue was so thick and clumpy on the table that I had to get out the sponge with the scratcher on one side. As I dunked that sponge into the scrub bucket, I realized that no matter how long I held it underwater, there was a limited amount of water it had the capacity to hold. Until I squeezed some out and spread it on the table, there was no room for more. It made me think of the little guy's words earlier that morning. God's love does go on forever, and if I squeeze out the love he lavishes on me and share it with others, he will be right there to fill me back up, just as I filled that sponge back up every time I dunked it in the bucket.

We often wonder how we can evangelize or share the Gospel message. I think it's like squeezing out the love God gave us all over others to make room for more. The love and mercy of the Father is tough for the human mind to understand, but it amazes me time and time again. The lepers Saint Marianne served were afflicted with a highly contagious disease, but she never feared it. She loved those in her care for thirty-five years and never contracted the disease. God allowed her to be his hands and agent of mercy and compassion until she died of natural causes at the age of eighty. Every time we go out of our way to share his love, he immediately fills us back up. He simply can't be outdone in generosity and love.

One week I was showered with a giant gush of God's love. I woke up Thursday with a giant headache, but I didn't want to miss school. During morning prayer, I lovingly promised that I would offer the suffering from my pounding head and queasy stomach for the benefit of my oldest son, who was taking college finals that day, and for a little boy battling cancer. I told God that every time I thought I wanted to complain, I would ask him to bless them instead. Later that morning, I received a surprise package from a sweet, thoughtful lady in our community. The gift was a beautiful bag designed to carry my Bible. It came with a notebook and pens, and, embroidered on the front of the bag in my favorite color, purple, it read, "Joyful Words." I was touched by that loving gift right down to the tip of my toes. As I admired the gift and wiped the tears from my eyes as I read her touching note, I realized my headache was gone. I offered the gift of my inconvenience and discomfort out of love for two others, and God blasted me back with a love even greater than I could have possibly given. He just can't be outdone. If you're not sure about that, give it a try. Give a giant heap of love away, and just see how God fills your sponge back up and the circle of his love continues on!

To grow in joyful love: Go out of your way this week to give a loving gift to another. It could be a gift of your time and talent or patience and prayer. Then sit back and take note of the blessings that come back to you.

St. Marianne Cope, pray for us!

6
Aggressive Tenderness

Christian triumph is always a cross, yet a cross which is at the same time a victorious banner borne with aggressive tenderness against the assaults of evil. — Pope Francis, Evangelii Gaudium *(On the Proclamation of the Gospel in Today's World)*

I sat squashed into a gym full of teenagers listening to an amazing, dynamic man named Justin Fatica. He began his talk by quoting the above words from Pope Francis, saying that the only way we are going to heal the ills of the world is to love each other with aggressive tenderness. I just can't get those words out of my head. It's hard to even imagine what this looks like, isn't it! It makes "do unto others" seem a little weak in comparison. As I've let these words tumble around in my head, I've been wondering what aggressive tenderness might be like.

It all became a little clearer a while later when I opened the children's Bible to the next story and read to my first graders. The story I opened to was about Jesus washing the feet of his apostles. That was aggressive tenderness. When we talked about the kind of shoes they wore and how there were no sidewalks or grass to walk on, the little lovelies began to realize it wasn't simply a foot rinse. That kind of dirty feet must have taken some scrubbing, they thought. Aggressive tenderness is digging deep. It's bigger than giving away old clothes and donating a few boxes of cereal to the food pantry. Becoming a person who loves in this way will take a lot of reflection and change.

We are so quick to judge and then apply kindness and tenderness according to our judgment. Saint Marianne loved the lepers not out of pity or duty but because they were God's beloved. While the world exiled them away from all the people and places they knew, she and her sisters loved them ferociously. She fought bureaucrats and budgets to bring them a life filled with faith, happiness, and laughter. She washed her eyes of what the world saw and put the intent of Jesus' teaching at the Last Supper into action.

I think the aggressive part means we have to desire to love like this, and we must be willing to work hard and tackle our attitudes and make a change. When I think of the word *tenderness*, I think of the way we treat a newborn. I remember my kids as babies. I would just watch them sleep in amazement and delight. I didn't love them less if they smelled bad, couldn't hold an intelligent conversation, or do anything to help me; I just loved them … because, and no matter what. Is it possible to love others like that? Mother Teresa did it, Saint Marianne did it, Pope Francis does it, and maybe we think we can't … but what if we tried a little harder?

If we really did love others with aggressive tenderness, what would we have to lose? Our reputation? Yeah, wouldn't you just hate to be thought of as a … loving person! Our relationships? What would that conversation sound like? "Gee, I just don't want to spend so much time with you anymore. You are just too loving and patient and you're always making others feel valued — I'm just not comfortable with all that." Our time? Are you kidding me; if we traded in all the minutes we spend judging people, talking about people, and complaining about stuff people do that bothers us, we might have way too much time on our hands and wind up doing something really nuts like praying for all those people instead. Our eternal life? Seriously, loving others with aggressive tenderness is exactly the way we can spend our days in the glory of eternal life. Who wants that? Oh, wait … I do … yikes! The excuses sound pretty lame, don't they?

Sometimes the best way to do something hard is to imagine how things would be if we already did it. If we loved with aggressive tenderness, suicide and substance abuse rates would plummet. The world would be filled with people who realized they were amazing because they were "wondrously made," leading to contentment, love, joy, peace, and more aggressive tenderness. We would be surrounded by people who see and value others as God's children and not as rich or poor, beautiful or ugly, smart or dumb, valuable or worthless. Aggressive tenderness allows us to look through the eyes of Christ. That sounds pretty amazing to me! Aggressive tenderness … who's ready?

To grow in joyful love: Every journey begins with a small step in the right direction. What is the first thing you're going to do to start loving with aggressive tenderness?

St. Marianne Cope, pray for us!

7
A Legend with a Lesson

He had no form or comeliness that we should look at him, and no beauty that we should desire him. — Isaiah 53:2

There are a lot of things I wish I were: thin, tall, better at math, more focused in silent prayer. On the other hand, there are a lot of things I'm glad I'm not: homeless, friendless, godless, or a mother pelican. Yup, you read that right … I'm glad I'm not a mama pelican. Before you think I'm nuts, let me tell you a story. The legend of the pelican may be old news to some, a beautiful reminder to many, or all new stuff to others. I've run across the legend of the pelican three times very recently, and three is a magic number for me. I always ask God to give me things three times if it's really important, so when the third reference to mama pelicans came to my attention, I knew right away he had an important idea to put on my heart. I am also aware that when he does this, it is almost always going to require repentance and change on my part, but I know the lesson will be taught with patience and devoted love from the teacher.

If you study a picture of a mama pelican, you will notice she has a blood-red tip to her beak. The legend says it's symbolic of a behavior: It was thought that when the mother couldn't find food for her young, she would thrust her beak into her own breast and allow her young to be fed from her very being, both her body and her blood. Talk about the ultimate self-sacrifice! What strikes me as truly amazing is that this particular bird is not noted for its beauty or performance in any way. It doesn't have a notable song or a sweetness that would make it a popular species. By many standards, pelicans would even be considered a nuisance without noble purpose. Does that description remind you of anyone?

Pelicans can be found in Church art because they symbolize the same kind of self-sacrificing love and bloodshed demonstrated by Jesus Christ himself. The blood of the New Covenant was shed to give each of us life, eternal life and life to the fullest. Like the pelican's emergency food supply, the gift comes from a surprise donor — not one of nobility and notoriety but one of humble, simple, and underestimated greatness.

How often we judge by appearance instead of by truly important standards and fail to see with the eyes of God! While we strive for fancy and sparkly things that will cause others to notice and admire us, Jesus invites us to accept and offer his love radically to everyone, without concern for their appearance or status. He tries to teach us daily that the opinion of the world will gain us nothing that will lead to our sainthood. The notice and approval of others is fleeting, while his love is self-emptying and everlasting. Holy actions should be our mission to bring glory to God, not to ourselves. In the words of Saint Marianne, "What little good we can do in this world to help and comfort, the suffering we wish to do it quietly and so far as possible, unnoticed and unknown."

The crucifix is a symbol of unfathomable love. We don't gaze on the crucifix or the image of a mama pelican because we have an attraction to things that are painful and gory. We reflect on them and pray with them because they serve as a reminder of the selfless love poured out for us, his children. Giving your own life in exchange for another is a sign of overwhelming love, and reflecting on this gift from the Father as we gaze at the crucifix should inspire us to live with gratitude and desire to celebrate and share the great news of his enormous love.

To grow in joyful love: In your prayer time this week, find an image of a pelican and a crucifix. Pray with both, pondering the great gift of self-sacrificing love they represent.

St. Marianne Cope, pray for us!

8
Love in Motion

Little children, let us not love in word or speech
but in deed and in truth. — 1 John 3:18

I love watching parents in action. I especially love when a mom or dad can immediately halt a behavior with just a look. You know, the look. No words needed, just the look. I find it really amazing when that look comes from a gentle, sweet little mom. I observed a tiny, mighty mom at work in the airport one day, and I'm telling you, as I got caught in the crosshairs of her gaze, I felt a chill, and I sat up straight myself! As fierce as that look was, it was done out of love for her squabbling boys, and it was so much better than ugly words or threats. I can only imagine what this world could become if we all took a cue from this line in Saint John's letter and focused on our deeds more than our words.

The first few words of this verse give us a mission: love. Love is so much more than sappy, kissy-face, gooey stuff. Hollywood gets it wrong, social media gets it wrong, and the news gets it wrong, so it's no wonder we're all a little fuzzy when it comes to figuring out what love really looks like! The kind of love Saint John writes about is the real-deal kind of love. Love is mercy, and mercy means forgiveness, and forgiveness means choosing the Father's way. Love allows us to see people as their creator sees them. When we look through his lens, love becomes giving, not taking. Love is not a suggestion; it's necessary to make earthly life meaningful and eternal life possible.

I don't know about you, but I could pray on this verse for weeks and probably still not get it right. We are told by the world to find our voice and use our words, but it seems as though it's all becoming a giant screaming match with everybody trying to out-talk the next guy. It's also a little tricky to navigate through all the words and messages and pick out the truth. Words can be twisted and misinterpreted, but actions are concrete and powerful. Before she went to care for the lepers, Saint Marianne helped found two Catholic hospitals in New York with the stipulation that they would offer care to anyone regardless of color, cultural background, beliefs, or station in life. She was a model of living God's love in truth and in deed. It was the work she was called to do — when we think about the loving things we can do for others, it's important to pay attention to where God is calling us to love. Most of us will not be called to build a hospital, start an orphanage, or open a school to serve forgotten children, but we are being asked to do simple things with great love.

Not long ago, I sat in a gorgeous huge old cathedral. I was captivated by the beauty, but I was more deeply touched watching the people and the way I saw this verse come to life. I watched the woman in front of me reach over to touch the shoulder of a hurting friend. No words were spoken, just a simple touch and a look steeped in compassion. As I gazed at the stunning stained-glass windows, I became distracted by a man who was using his necktie to play peekaboo with the restless toddler in front of him whose mom was trying desperately to hold on to his wiggly body. As I listened to the bishop of the Diocese of Salt Lake City deliver a powerful homily, my gaze shifted to the usher as he welcomed a disheveled and frazzled-looking little old woman, taking her frail arm and escorting her to a seat. She wore years of worry on her brow, but as that usher put out his arm and led her to an empty seat, you could see the look of gratitude and peace on her face as she settled in. As I left the cathedral, I noticed the little house next door that served sandwiches to the city's homeless every day. God gave me a line from Scripture during Mass and then illustrated it for me in living color. I love it when he makes it so easy to see! Maybe today is a good day to just be quiet and do something. Loving deeds speak louder than words … so let's get busy!

To grow in joyful love: Spend a couple days praying with this verse and ask God to put people in your path who need a little action-packed quiet love!

St. Marianne Cope, pray for us!

9
Love Me Tender

And be kind to one another, tenderhearted, forgiving one another, as God in Christ forgave you. — Ephesians 4:32

"Love me tender, love me true ..." Raise your hand if you now have that old Elvis song stuck in your head. (If you're too young to know the song, Google it!) That 1956 hit created an image of a love dripping with sweetness that melted hearts, made females swoon, and prompted people to see love differently. The key word in that song was *tender*, and after this song topped the charts, the word then applied to more than just steak!

Remember Pope Francis and his encouragement to "love with aggressive tenderness"? Pope Francis spoke to a crowd early in his papacy and pointed to the tenderness of Saint Joseph, encouraging all Christians to imitate his loving tenderness. We usually define tenderness as "gentleness" or "kindness," or "sensitivity to pain." It seems a pretty great thing to be, doesn't it? In my mind there is something significantly different about treating someone nicely and treating someone tenderly. I'm telling you — this word has caused me to do a lot of thinking. I was washing dishes the other night thinking about all this tenderness stuff, and I glanced at the table and noticed a prayer book lying there.

When I finished, I opened it up and read a page about a man named Saint Poemen, an abbot who lived in the fifth century. I sat down on the porch and read this short page and wondered, "Where is this going, God?" As I got to the last paragraph, a story was told about a young brother who asked Poemen what should be done with someone who nods off during prayer. I often do this, so I was curious about the reply! The saint answered, "For my part, when I see a brother who is dozing, I put his head on my knees and let him rest."

Nothing like an old song and a really old holy guy to slam you with a lesson! There really isn't any better word to describe Poemen's response than *tenderness*. I sat there on the porch wondering if I had ever really shown true tenderness. I immediately saw my children as babies. I remembered lots of instances when I was tender to those three little people. I don't recall ever entering the baby room at three in the morning and screeching, "Knock it off; just suck it up and go back to sleep; I don't care how wet your diaper is or how hungry you are!" I would never have done that; I just sleepily picked them up, comforted them, and took care of them lovingly, tenderly, because they needed me. Then I wondered why I didn't look at others with the same tenderness. The big question became how the world would be different if we were all more tender. What if our first thought was "What do you need to feel better?" not "What is your problem?"

God is so tender with us, and so often I forget to tell him thank you for that. I suppose the best way of all to thank him is to love others with more tenderness. Treating others with tenderness isn't something we should do to be noticed. It is a true act of humility, and humility is the foundation of our sainthood because it inspires us to do all things for his glory! Saint Marianne often told her sisters, "Let us make the very best use of the precious moments and do all in our power for his dear sake and for his greater honor and glory." That seems like solid advice and great motivation for growing in tenderness.

As I was packing school lunches, asking God if working for more tenderness was really what he was asking me, I heard the sound of an insurance commercial coming from the TV in the living room. The theme song for the commercial was "Love Me Tender." You just can't make this stuff up, so I hope God stirs up something big in your heart with the word *tenderness*.

To grow in joyful love: Write the word *tenderness* on a sticky note and give it some thought and prayer this week. See where the Lord leads you.

St. Marianne Cope, pray for us!

The Second Gift

Joyful Suffering

10
St. Pio of Pietrelcina

Suffering, no matter how difficult it may be, when compared to the good that is accomplished, makes every pain a joy for the soul. — Padre Pio

A typical five-year-old wants fruit snacks, toys, and someone to play with. It's safe to say that St. Pio of Pietrelcina, knows as Padre Pio, was not a typical five-year-old because, at that age, he consecrated himself to Jesus and was guided by an overwhelming desire to serve God. His love of the Father and his mission to serve were so sincere and so intense that before the age of ten, his parents were helping him find a way to become a Capuchin friar, and about the time most young people are focused on getting their driver's license, Padre Pio began his life as a Capuchin.

The grace of such profound and unwavering devotion to Jesus was exactly the armor Padre Pio would cling to as his vocation became a beautiful tapestry of suffering, love, and humility offered to God. The story of his life is full of astounding events and accomplishments. He had the gift of reading souls, and he would often spend twelve to fifteen hours each day hearing confessions. Often as someone in the midst of great suffering offered his sins to the Lord, the smell of flowers would waft from Padre Pio's compartment of the confessional. He also had the gift of bilocation, and there were reports of military pilots in World War II witnessing a "flying friar" who prevented enemy bombs from being dropped. This saintly man had the gift of healing, and again and again, he compassionately, generously, and lovingly shared himself with Christ's suffering Church.

Some might wonder how one man was capable of all the astonishing events that make up this saint's story, but I think Padre Pio himself would be quick to point out that it was not him but Christ working through him by the merits of his suffering. He experienced poor health from early on and throughout his life, and the intensity of his physical suffering magnified. He bore the stigmata, the wounds of the crucified Christ, which he received not only in appearance but also in the intensity of the pain suffered by Jesus. He was so grateful that this suffering was given to him, and he embraced it as an opportunity to share in the suffering of Jesus. He suffered this pain for fifty years and offered it continuously for the salvation of God's people. As devout and humble as his life was, he suffered persecution — he was even accused of inflicting the wounds himself. This beloved saint also suffered from constant spiritual attacks yet never complained or wavered in his devotion and gratitude to the Father.

We often grow impatient in times of suffering and can find ourselves as squirmy as a toddler in church, but God is right there with us leading us to the joy that flows from the suffering. During our suffering, God is working in us and through us, and it's an amazing and joyful thing to realize we get to play a wee little part in the Father's work when we offer him our sufferings. What a joy to realize we are cooperating with him, and what a joy to see the ways he is strengthening, healing, and building hope.

At Padre Pio's death, the wounds were miraculously healed,

leaving no scars. His whole life was a lesson in joyful suffering, and it unveils again and again the mighty power of God to meet us in our suffering and bring unimaginable good from unthinkable sorrow and struggle. Just like the wounds this saint suffered, all of our wounds will be healed without a trace by the Father who loves us when we invite him into our suffering and offer it lovingly for his glory. Padre Pio was a living example of the words he spoke often: "The greater your suffering, the greater God's love for you." Padre Pio, we pray for your intercession to help us live out our sufferings with joy.

Padre Pio, pray for us!

11
A Big Question

For my thoughts are not your thoughts,
neither are your ways my ways, says the Lord. — *Isaiah 55:8*

As a teacher, I get asked a lot of questions every day. Everything from "Is it almost time for lunch?" to "Why do people say mean, stupid things?" Sometimes I have an answer because the question is routine or simple; often, I'm left asking the Holy Spirit for words because I simply don't know. After one of my recent speaking events, a beautiful soul sent a question I didn't know quite how to answer. I was neck-deep in Holy Week and Easter stuff at school, so I could have typed a quick reply in an attempt to take the task off my to-do list, but the question begged prayerful thought, research, and, of course, the wisdom of God's word. What started as an email to answer a question has become something bigger, because I'm sure this dear lady isn't the only one who has this wonder. With the help of the Holy Spirit, Scripture, and a dynamic priest, here's what I've got.

The question sprang from a Scripture verse I was talking about that night in a church hall. We were thinking about Psalm 139:13–14, which reads, "You knitted me together in my mother's womb. / I praise you, for I am wondrously made." It's a beautiful passage steeped in God's loving truth. But sometimes it comes with a sting. What if we aren't perfect? What if we're sick, or we have a condition or situation that causes our life to be anything but wonderful and perfect? Did God knit that? When life is hard or confusing, or the suffering is huge, we often turn to God in our pain and befuddlement and wonder where he is. Did he really intend things to be this way?

Here are a couple of things to think about. First of all, there is no such thing as perfect. The world peddles that concept constantly, but it's a deception. There is no such thing as a perfect family, job, or life like the TV commercials would have us believe. The goal of life is to get to heaven, not to have everything neat, tidy, pretty, and easy. The goal of life is to get to heaven and claim our sainthood — and, my friends, the path to that is not so simple. The holy men and women who have gone before us have shown us again and again that the path to holiness requires sacrifice and suffering. In John's Gospel we read the words "In the world you have tribulation" (16:33). Even though hard stuff comes with a warning label, we still shake our fist and say, "What the heck, God!" We have to know that he hears us, he loves us, and he is working right in the middle of the messy, imperfect, and unwonderful parts of our life. He's using them to bring us to holiness and lead us home. Sometimes that's a quick trip, but more often than not, it's a long journey.

The second thing to remember is that suffering is inevitable. There are hundreds of commercials out there for stuff to make things quicker or easier. Heaven just plain can't happen without suffering and trial; there's no short-cut. What we do with our suffering makes all the difference. Suffering without Jesus is just pain without a purpose, and it can leave us bitter and fumbling in the darkness. Suffering united with Jesus brings holiness. Saint Paul said in the Letter to the Colossians, "Now I rejoice in my sufferings for your sake" (1:24). His words are even more powerful when you consider that he wrote them while chained in a prison cell. Paul knew the secret. He knew that Jesus died on a cross not to take away our suffering but rather to transform our suffering. If we say in our suffering, "Jesus, please suffer with me; please allow this thing to help me grow closer to you," we will give our suffering purpose, and the result is redemption. In other words, suffering is our vehicle to heaven. Uniting our suffering with Jesus gives our suffering meaning and gets us closer to that wonderful, perfect life we're all working for.

If suffering is our "vehicle" to heaven, it's helpful to note that no two look alike. We buy into the crazy notion that everything should be fair — yet another deception of the world. When Christ allows us to carry a sliver of his cross, we grow in holiness and often help others through our personal suffering. It might be tempting to think it's not fair because some sufferings seem much smaller or greater, but the reality is that God knows exactly how much we can bear. My mom suffered greatly when she buried my twenty-three-year-old brother and then again a year later when she began her losing battle with cancer, but she always asked God to use that suffering not just for her soul but for that of her husband, her children, and all those who needed the redemption her suffering might bring to them. Padre Pio offered these words of wisdom to those who were in the midst of suffering: "Stay in the boat in which he placed you and let the storm come. He may sleep, but at the opportune time he will awake to restore your calm." We can never completely see the burdens that others might be bearing. Only God can see them, and we have to trust in his wisdom and mercy.

That was a rather long answer to a pretty big question. I hope it offers some peace, some understanding, and … maybe some hope.

To grow in joyful suffering: As you pray today, make a list of all the things that cause your heart suffering. Each time that thing enters your mind, say, "Jesus, join me as I carry this sliver of your cross."

Padre Pio, pray for us!

12
Cracks, Chips, and Leaks

Yet, O L*ORD*, *you are our Father;*
we are the clay, and you are our potter;
we are all the work of your hand. — *Isaiah 64:8*

I can close my eyes and see it sitting there on the top shelf of the cupboard above the plates and cereal bowls. I couldn't reach it, so it was always someone else's job to put it away after I had carefully dried it. It was a turquoise-blue glass casserole dish, the only one my mom had, and she treasured it. My dad had given it to her for Christmas, and if she pulled it out to use for supper, we knew she was going to be making something special. One day when I was about ten, I came home from school, and Mom was on her way to a meeting. She asked me to put the casserole dish in the oven at five o'clock. I felt so important! I quickly raced to the kitchen and peeked under the glass lid to see what she had assembled inside the dish. It was beautiful; it looked like something you'd see in a cookbook picture. Well, the appointed time came, I opened the oven door, and, as I lifted the casserole dish up to slide it into the oven, it slipped right out of my hands, crashed to the floor, and shattered into pieces. I didn't even consider the fact that I had just ruined supper. I just felt awful about breaking her casserole dish.

I managed to clean up the mess before Mom got home, and I even began to prepare a Plan B supper. However, the hardest task of all was to hand Mom that collection of broken glass. She stared at it in silence for a moment, asked me if I was OK, and then said: "Well, now it's time to get creative. Your dad and brothers will be hungry, and it's almost time to eat." That was it ... no scolding, no lecture, no disappointed glance. It was just time to get creative and move on.

A few decades later, father began his homily with the words "God loves broken vessels!" My mind immediately rushed back to our kitchen in Hoyt, Kansas, when I was ten, staring down at that mangled mess of turquoise-colored glass and casserole. My mom's words echoed in my mind: "It's time to get creative." We are each lovingly crafted vessels made perfectly by the hands of a compassionate potter. When we sin, and when we are in the midst of great suffering, it's as if our vessels become chipped or cracked or leaky. I don't know about you, but I've managed to put some real dings in my vessel over the years. If you get a crack or a leak in your favorite mug or dish, it no longer functions the way it was intended to. When we sin, or rail against our suffering, we separate ourselves from Jesus, causing us to drift a bit from the Father's love. Just like that broken vessel, we don't function quite the way we were intended to. Padre Pio had a great affinity for those who suffered and felt broken. He was so passionate in sharing the message of the Lord's desire to restore and mend our brokenness that he founded a special hospital for the relief of the suffering. His desire was to help people embrace their brokenness and allow souls to use it as a bridge to the Father's healing love.

Luckily, we are more valuable than mugs without a handle or casserole dishes shattered into dozens of pieces. The Father is never going to throw us out! Instead, he uses our weakness to demonstrate his strength. If we have a chip or a leak, he invites us to come to him and give him a chance to restore us, to make us strong and purposeful again. He is the potter that created us. We are the work of his hands. So, if we need to be restored and have our purpose renewed, all we have to do is ask him, and he will create us anew … as many times as we need it! God loves broken vessels because they require his strength, and any time we give him the opportunity to show his strength by admitting our weakness and inviting him right into the middle of our suffering, we are blessed with his strength and grace.

To grow in joyful suffering: Identify a chip or a leak in your vessel caused by suffering and ask God to strengthen and restore that imperfection in your life. Pick a different one tomorrow and a new one after that, but don't forget to make a list of the blessings you receive as the potter lovingly restores your vessel.

Padre Pio, pray for us!

13
The Tenth Month

Love is patient and kind; love is not jealous or boastful; it is not arrogant or rude. — 1 Corinthians 13:4–5

October, the tenth month, is my favorite month of the year! I always get a little giddy when it's time to flip the calendar from September to October, and a little blue when it's time to flip from October to November. I love everything about October: the weather, the colors, the smells, and the tastes. Let's face it, you can buy apple cider any time of the year, but it tastes better fresh from the orchard in October! It's fun when it starts to get cooler, and you get the box from the storeroom that has the sweaters and sweatshirts in it — it's like shopping for free, and everything seems new. The tenth month is home to the greatest sufferings and the greatest joys in my life, and through these events, this verse from 1 Corinthians comes to life.

A few decades ago, on October 5, I married the greatest guy *ever*! His love for me and our children and grandchildren overwhelms me on a regular basis! He's gentle and kind and humble and honest, to name just a few of his attributes, all demonstrated in his quiet, inconspicuous way. It's the understatement of the century to say that he is the biggest blessing

God ever plopped in my lap. Through this blessing came three more blessings. Words can't even describe how amazing it is to see how God can multiply the love you have in your heart and make it big enough to share with everyone in your house ... even when they've just trampled on your last nerve and eaten all but the last five Cheerios and put the box back in the cupboard! I guess that's where the "love is patient" part comes in. I love my life! My family, my home, my job, my church, my town, all of it — but I'm reminded in the tenth month of each year that it was one of the saddest Octobers that allowed God to lead me to all these blessings.

Early in the month, almost forty Octobers ago, at the age of forty-six, my mom lost her battle with brain cancer. She was teaching and loving right up till the end. During those last few weeks of her fight, she would ask me to hand her the wooden box that contained her collection of notecards so that she could write thank you notes to people who had touched her life or helped her family. She'd ask me to finish some of them for her, but I had to promise to use only the words she told me to use. She said everyone deserved to know about it if they were appreciated. In those notes, she would point out something lovely about that person, like her smile or his friendly nature. She spent those last weeks being anything but rude, bitter, or inflated.

I asked her one day if she ever asked God, "Why me?" She honestly admitted that she had asked that question a couple of times, but she said the better question was "Why not me?" I can still hear her voice say, "What makes me think I'm so special that something hard and sad and painful shouldn't happen to me?" Now that was "Love is not jealous" in action. She often said throughout her journey that heaven was for the shiniest souls and suffering is God's way of shining us up. She reminded me that one of my childhood tasks was helping her shine the family's church shoes on Saturday afternoon so that they would be ready for Mass on Sunday: "Our suffering and struggle on earth is to heaven what the shoe polish and brush were to our shoes." Every time I walk past a shoe-shine bench in an airport, I think of that lesson!

Many Octobers later, I see how the sad connects to the happy so flawlessly that only God could have done it. See, the truth is that I loved my mother with all my heart, and I don't think I would have moved eight hundred miles away to Michigan if she were still in Kansas. God knew. He knew that the sad chapter in my life would have an amazingly happy ending. He's that good, and he's that loving! He even handled the travel arrangements that got me to Michigan. Through it all, I have learned to trust because I have seen and felt the way God cares for us in elaborate and intricate detail.

Recognizing God's love means understanding that you have the experiences in your life in God's perfect time, for good reason … and they are your experiences. Don't be jealous of another person's life because it seems easier than your own. You don't know what you don't know. God's got a journey for each of us, and we can't look jealously at the blessings or "good life" of others, because we have no idea what strife and suffering might have led them to it. Imitating the pure love of God means celebrating blessings and comforting sorrows with all those God puts in our path. Life on earth is a delicate balance of both! The works of the Father aren't predictable to the human way of thinking. Something that seems horrible to us, like Padre Pio's stigmata, changed the faith of thousands of people. As persistently painful as those marks were, they radiated a floral perfume that was sweet and peaceful. God is constantly wedged in with both the good and the bad. October is my favorite, but no matter what day or month it is, run out and love somebody in 1 Corinthians 13:4 style today!!!

To grow in joyful suffering: Follow my mom's example of loving kindness and send a note of thanks or appreciation to somebody who has touched your life. For extra credit, send it handwritten and mailed with a stamp! Trading your suffering and struggle for an act of love for another helps put things in beautiful perspective.

Padre Pio, pray for us!

14
Not What I Expected

In the world you have tribulation; but be of good cheer, I have overcome the world. — John 16:33

When the "three little Wohlferts" were all in school, I went back to school and turned my Kansas secondary teaching certificate into a Michigan elementary teaching certificate. Some days were way more amazing than I ever expected, and other days not what I expected at all! My first teaching partner taught me more about being a good elementary teacher during my first semester than I learned in all my years of college. She loved her job, she was great at her job, and she had an amazing ability to draw the best from each student and "get the job done." She affectionately referred to me as "Pollyanna." I will admit I am like that character because I usually live in my little bubble, always thinking things are going to be just fine and just as lovely as I see them in my mind.

But sometimes life takes a turn from the way I've pictured how it should be, and this Pollyanna gets her britches in a twist. Suffering often catches us by surprise, and I don't know too many folks who wind up in a rough patch and give a big "Yippee! Bring it on!" Most of us get ruffled, rattled, and angry and do just about anything we can think of to wiggle out of it.

The older I get, the more I am reminded that life is about balance. If we go through life expecting things to always be happy or right or good, there will be trouble, and we will get frustrated. As I look back at the twists and turns in my life, I realize it was those times when stuff I didn't expect landed in my lap that were the times when I grew and changed and deepened my trust in God the most.

We tend to get a little hung up on good stuff. When things are good and happy, we expect them to stay that way — and then when the unexpected happens, we can feel a little as though we've been punished or abandoned by the Father who is supposed to love us. As a society, we can be pretty "all or nothing" in our thinking. We forget that nothing but heaven is meant to be permanent. Not happiness, and certainly not sorrow. God works through both the good times and the tough times. We can be assured of his blessings and his love always! He did not suggest there might be trouble. He didn't say perhaps on the third Thursday of July there is a chance you will have trouble. No, he flat out promised that trouble would happen. So why are we so puzzled and pouty when it does?

I think it's usually because we weren't expecting it. I don't suppose Padre Pio expected to leave school to care for the family sheep herd when hard times came to his family. I don't think he expected to miss three years of school and fall behind in his studies. But God is bigger than our expectations and has a brilliant plan for our lives. His plan honored Pio's sacrifice when his father was able to get work in America so that they could afford a tutor to catch the soon-to-be friar up in time to enter the monastery. God's good grace and mercy are far beyond and far superior to our expectations.

Each time I come through troubles, I feel stronger and more peaceful. The greatest thing trouble does for me is make me realize that compared to most other folks … I've got nothin'! It makes me realize I have so much to be thankful for and so many reasons to praise his Holy Name! I read a little slogan on a billboard not long ago that fits perfectly. The sign said, "Don't let your troubles get you down. Remember, you can't use an egg unless it's broken."

Maybe it's the Pollyanna in me, but I believe that even in my biggest troubles, I can look back and truly see the hand of God guiding and protecting me. Nothing is without reason … and we may not always like the reason, but it is exactly in those situations when I just have to sigh, shrug my shoulders, and say, "This must be something I need for heaven." Life is full of things I didn't expect. I didn't expect to move to Michigan, I didn't expect to teach elementary school, and I certainly didn't expect to be a writer! I didn't expect to get gray hair or have reading glasses perpetually perched on my head, and I certainly didn't expect every dessert I ate to become a permanent part of my lower torso! However, in each of those unexpected events, there have been great blessings. We are going to be judged not on what we expected but rather on how we managed the unexpected.

To grow in joyful suffering: Where is Christ working in your life? Look hard at the tough stuff and see where he's walking with you.

Padre Pio, pray for us!

15
No Explanation Required

Jesus answered, "It was not that this man sinned, or his parents, but that the works of God might be made manifest in him." — John 9:3

We like explanations, don't we? Our world surrounds us with technology, information, and knowledge designed to explain and justify everything … until we hit one of those rough patches that we simply can't make sense of. We aren't so good at meaning the words "That's just the way it is." We demand proof! We are a society of highly intelligent humans, after all — there should be a way to describe, defend, and understand everything. If there isn't, then somebody must have lied or done something wrong, because all things should make sense! If things don't make sense, or if we don't like the explanation we've been given, we set out looking for a spot to lay the blame. The more out-of-balance our society's moral compass becomes, the harder it is to accept things we can't explain — earthly suffering and God's work included.

After reading this passage from John's Gospel, I guess the game of prove or blame isn't new. The disciples were busy trying to figure out why the blind man was afflicted. They wanted to lay blame or find fault in order to understand the situation, but Jesus explained the answer in a simple yet completely profound way. The blind man's affliction or suffering was not intended to punish or to penalize; his situation was meant to magnify the amazing power of God. I've listened to this reading a dozen times before, and I always thought of that man who lived on the streets in darkness with pity and sadness. After some time in prayer, I saw him with different eyes, and I heard the story with different ears. My feelings for this gospel character turned from pity to something more like desire. God chose the blind man in such a pitiful state to show his glory — what a wonderful turn of events for him!

This Gospel reminded me of a conversation I had recently with a woman who just bubbles over with God's love. She was speaking so tenderly about her brother who had recently lost his battle with cancer. She shared her admiration and inspiration as she told his story. The part of the conversation that sunk deep into my heart was his reaction to the doctor's proclamation of his condition — difficult news, to say the least. Upon hearing the news, he told his sister how lucky he felt that God wanted him home in heaven at such an early age. As tears stung my eyes, it was easy to see why he was such an inspiration to her. There was no blame, no need for explanation … it was simply a case of accepting a situation of suffering as the work of the Father.

The trouble with trying to explain and understand everything is that we can only do it through the lens of human knowledge. Padre Pio had the gift of bilocation and was also seen levitating while in the midst of deep and peaceful prayer. Even though other friars witnessed these amazing sights, many didn't believe it could be possible. God is the one with the wisdom and understanding to see how things are woven together from beginning to end. We are only capable of seeing what's right in front of us, while God sees so much more. He knows the purpose for each situation and the potential refinement of our soul with each suffering. He knows what each event will prepare us for. He knows what will follow each disappointment and sadness. He knows the mighty and glorious ending to all our stories.

If we are willing to accept the happy ending we so desperately long for, then we need to remember that his job is to prepare us for it. Sickness, death, disappointment, and afflictions aren't meant to punish; they are meant to strengthen and renew and allow him to show his mighty and powerful love for his children. In our weakness, he shows his strength. That is the only explanation or understanding we ever need — it's as simple as that! The glory of his works on the other side of our struggle is more amazing than we can even begin to imagine. I believe this with all my heart because that's how much he loves us. So, the next time you're in the middle of yuck, remind yourself that God is the only justification, understanding, and explanation you need. Remind yourself that the glory he will show through your strife will be every bit as magnificent as the way the blind man felt the moment he washed the mud from his eyes and could see for the first time. Remember that God's ways are not our ways. His are best, and they don't require explanation or understanding, just our trust!

To grow in joyful suffering: Read John 9 and make a list of situations where you need to surrender your suffering. Pause trying to understand, justify, and explain and simply ask God to make you aware of the ways he's working in them.

Padre Pio, pray for us!

16
Addition, Subtraction, and Holiness

He must increase, but I must decrease. — John 3:30

How's that for a piece of Scripture that stands in complete opposition to today's culture? We aren't big fans of sacrificing things we want or enjoy or that we prefer to control. We certainly don't often entertain the notation of sacrificing our stuff in favor of having less. Everywhere we turn, someone is trying to market something to give us more. More money, more beauty, more power … you name it, somebody's selling it, and many Americans are lining up to buy it. All the while, the Father who loves us gently suggests less of our stuff and more of him. His words contain the promise that if we make a sacrifice and choose his way, we will be blessed beyond measure. This is a passage that has come to me again and again, and I've done a beautiful job of ignoring it! Poor God, sometimes he has to work so much harder to get my attention than he should have to! I'm not a big fan of math, but in this verse, God has given us a pretty simple equation to follow: Add more of him; subtract some of our plans, desires, and control; and the answer equals holiness.

Every teacher's summer begins the same, with a long list of chores that need to be done because I didn't get to them during the school year. These tasks are real gems — things like cleaning closets, extracting the crumbs from the silverware drawer, or washing windows and blinds! This summer I had lots of other things on my list too: great books to read, letters to write, and sitting on the porch. I told myself none of the fun stuff until the yucky stuff was done. So I started with the easy tasks and procrastinated on some of the really awful ones. It got to the point that I dug in my heels and practically threw a hissy fit about the last few jobs on my list. I didn't want to sacrifice lovely summer days for yucky chores, and it was making me crabby, and I was ashamed of my procrastination.

As I was doing morning prayers one morning, the devotional talked about offering our most "undesirable tasks," including suffering over them, as a loving gift to the Lord, making the tasks more about him and less about self. Hmm … that was aimed right at me, and it was a great idea, but I decided to fold a load of laundry before I tackled those awful jobs. As I was folding, I reached into the basket and pulled out Shannon's red T-shirt from Bible study. The back of the shirt read, "He must increase, I must decrease. John 3:30." As if that wasn't strange enough, I don't remember Shannon even wearing that shirt in the past month, yet there it was in the laundry that day! I was beginning to soften a bit, so I dropped to my knees and said, "OK God, I'll do these awful, gross, not-fun-at-all chores out of love for you and in thanksgiving for all you've blessed me with. More of you, less of me." One second after I said amen and pulled myself off the floor, Jason walked in and said, "Mom, do you need anything?" He helped me with three of the worst jobs on the list, and we finished much faster than I had planned.

Suffering, struggling, and disappointment are real, and they touch all of us. In the words of Padre Pio, "The Lord sometimes makes you feel the weight of the cross. Although the weight seems intolerable, you are able to carry it, because the Lord, in his love and mercy, extends a hand to you and gives you strength." Sometimes our prayer is straight-up subtraction: Lord, take away this suffering. We want him to add convenience and comfort to our daily life. But the more we are willing to let go of our worldly notions and expectations, the more he multiplies his grace and his love for us. Holiness just isn't possible without his grace and his love. So, the formula one more time: I must decrease, and he must increase.

To grow in joyful suffering: Take three opportunities this week to deliberately put this verse into action.

Padre Pio, pray for us!

17
Joy in the Trials

Count it all joy, my brethren, when you meet with various trials, for you know that the testing of your faith produces steadfastness. — James 1:2–3

Count trials as joy? What was Saint James thinking when he wrote this? Upon first glance at this verse, we might be tempted to wonder if the beloved saint put in a few too many prayerful all-nighters. Surely he wasn't serious about feeling joyful when the washer breaks, someone you love gets sick, the fuel pump on the car goes out, or the sweet teenager in your home eats the last piece of peach pie you were hiding … I mean saving … in the back of the fridge! Joy? I don't think so! And what about the really big stuff like losing your job or serious illness? Surely he couldn't have meant those things could bring joy.

We could sit down and make a list of all the trials that have happened upon us in the past month, and we would be overcome with many emotions, none of which would be joy! Amid our struggles and sufferings, no matter how big or how small, we need to remind ourselves that joy and happiness are different. Joy is being in the will of the Father, and sometimes that's a tough place to be … but the joy comes in knowing he's walking through the suffering with us, and he's giving it meaning and purpose.

The real meat of this verse is the part that explains what we can get in exchange for our trials: stronger faith and steadfastness, or, in another translation, perseverance. Do you remember when you were young and came home from school complaining about that boy who pulled your pigtails or the girl who annoyingly pointed out your every move to the teacher? The standard reply from home went something like this: "Well, honey, if they didn't like you, they wouldn't tease you." This verse has a little bit of that flavor to it, don't you think? God promised that we would have trouble — it is a guarantee, not a possibility. Even though we've read those words more than once, trials still seem to catch us by surprise. We sometimes even cop an attitude and think, "What, me … why me, Lord? What have I done to deserve this difficulty?" We might even get really sassy and say, "Oh, pardon me, Father, but you've made a mistake; I've already had eight serious trials this month. I believe this current dilemma belongs to the neighbor or, even better, the guy who cut me off in traffic this morning!" Growing in sainthood requires us to do hard things. Thankfully that is exactly why God so freely gives us the gift of his grace: so that we can lean on him to grow and change from a worldly perspective to a godly one.

Holiness often brings tasks that are tough or menial, but we are called to obey and follow God's plan. Padre Pio would very often hear confessions for twelve to fifteen hours a day. I can't even imagine such a task, but this beautiful saint was given the grace and the joy to complete it and to cherish the privilege of offering the mercy of Christ. The Father sustained Padre Pio with the energy and passion he needed to love all the beloved souls who came to confession.

The simple truth is that if God didn't love us, he wouldn't give us trials at all. Each difficulty or disappointment that knocks on our front door or barges right into our day is an opportunity to grow in trust or compassion or patience. When we throw up our hands in despair and say, "OK, God, I don't know how to do this; I don't think I'm strong enough for this. Please guide me and guard me and love me through it," we will grow in faith and perseverance. Plus, we will be blessed with grace and mercy. I think what Saint James is teaching us is that any time we surrender to the holy power of God, that's joyful, and the blessing we receive is more strength, more grace, and more faith for the next thing! It seems strange to thank God for the lousy stuff, but that is what we are called to do. We need to act as if we are completely aware that he is about to do a mighty work through our trial if we just stand back and let him take us through it.

To grow in joyful suffering: The next time a trial comes your way, stop and thank God for it and ask him to show you the joy in the situation.

Padre Pio, pray for us!

18
But Why

I have said this to you, that in me you may have peace. — John 16:33

I've been doing a lot of thinking lately about all the people knee-deep in lousy stuff. I have gotten many emails and texts from people who need prayer to navigate their way through life. There is sickness, distress, and family and job difficulties, and some of these requests are swirling really close to home. I'm so happy they ask for prayer, and I've been praying my little tail off. Absolutely I trust, I believe, and my faith is strong as a boulder, but every now and again I just want to say, "Hey, wait a doggone minute, God! This is all too much!" I'm sure that comment during my prayer is followed by a heavenly facepalm!

The big question I've been hearing from those folks struggling is "If God loves us, why does this lousy stuff happen?" I would have to say that's a completely fair question, and I wish like heck I could type an answer to make it all better, but here is the truth. For one thing, God doesn't make bad stuff happen, and he loves us even harder when it does. And sometimes, there isn't a simple answer to complicated things. I've spent some time praying and thinking, and here are some of the things that made me feel better.

There is a big difference between being involved and being in control. God is completely involved in our lives, and the more we pray and grow in our relationship with him, the more involved he will be. Because of our free will, God does not control our lives. Some of the distress I've been asked to pray for is the result of someone doing something lousy with his or her free will and leaving others to suffer in the wake of poor choices. God isn't in control of that, but he can absolutely be involved in our lives as we navigate through it, if we invite him to meet us there and lead us through. He won't wave a magic wand and make it all disappear, but he will give us the grace and the strength to endure the difficulties if we ask. Padre Pio used to offer these wise words to those who were struggling: "Today reach up as high as you can and God will reach down the rest of the way."

God doesn't give people cancer or trap children in a cave because his "master plan" indicated it was time for it. That is not how a loving Father operates. If a dad decided to go for a walk with his son, and along the way the son stepped in a gopher hole and hurt his ankle, that would be a lousy thing. Lousy as it is, the dad didn't make it happen. He was absolutely there, but he didn't plan it or want it to happen; he wasn't in control of it, but you can bet your bottom dollar that he instantly became involved. He felt the hurt, he poured out compassion and comfort, and he did everything possible to aid in his son's healing.

If God controlled everything, we might think life would be easier and fear, suffering, and pain would be long gone. I suppose in some ways that makes sense, but because of our sinful nature (thank you, Adam, Eve, and Satan) we want what we want. And we aren't always so good at trusting and following the rules, let alone being completely controlled, so this idea has some holes. God doesn't force his love or his perfect will on us. It's up to us to choose to love, trust, surrender, and follow him. When we're tempted to think God makes bad things happen, it's good to remember a few truths from Scripture. Jesus heals the sick; he doesn't bring about their illness. Jesus liberates the oppressed; he doesn't prolong their oppression. Jesus sets the prisoner free; he doesn't imprison. Jesus restores a broken creation; he doesn't further cripple it through disease, suffering, and pain.

When I find myself feeling overwhelmed about the sadness or madness of a lousy situation, I have to reach for the three biggest truths of all. They're stiff ones, and sometimes they go down like vinegar, but they are enormous truths spoken in even bigger love. First, every situation, no matter how sad or tragic or difficult, is one where God can bring about a greater good. The part that makes that really tough to wrap our heads and hearts around is that sometimes we hurt too much to see the good, and often the greater good is for someone else. Second, Scripture says there will be trouble, and it is only through suffering we can fully come to Christ. When I realize that and stop to contemplate the suffering both the Father and the Son have experienced for me, it really puts things in perspective. Finally, Heaven is the reward, not earth. As humans, we cling to the familiar and fear the unknown. If we could begin to unwrap even a tiny corner of the delight, glory, and absolute magnificence of eternal life, we would run from this world so fast we'd be nothing but a streak!

The lousy stuff is never what we wish for, but there is love, healing, and even salvation when we truly let the Father get involved and walk with us through the lousy. The lousy stuff is where God shows his power, his compassion, and his amazing ability to unite, support, and draw people closer to each other and to heaven.

To grow in joyful suffering: Spend some time asking God to be involved in your struggles or the struggles of someone you love. Trust him and then watch to see the way he works.

Padre Pio, pray for us!

The Third Gift
Joyful Trust

19
Bl. Anne-Marie Javouhey

I am in God's hands, ready to do God's Will as soon as it is revealed to me. — Bl. Anne-Marie Javouhey

Trust is a funny thing. In our human nature, we put it in a small box and apply it most often to things and people we can be fairly certain are trustworthy. It's easy to trust things like a car that starts or a chair that will withstand our sitting, but the joyful trust we're truly called to requires us to look bigger, dig deeper, and stretch further. We can easily trust in the providence of God when we have extra money tucked away, but to truly trust in the Lord, we must surrender everything — our stuff, our plans, and our control — in exchange for the will of the Father. Growing in trust requires humility tangled up with a big splash of truth because when we don't trust, we're stuck with the silly notion that we know what to do and how to do it, and the Father's plan is simply a reference point or a resource. When we trust the creator wholeheartedly, there is no second guessing or plan B, and we simply rest with joy in our heart knowing nothing in our life is too big, scary, or painful for the one who created the entire universe.

Blessed Anne-Marie experienced true trust and joyful faith

as a young French girl, though her carefree life changed drastically during the French Revolution. She trusted God to help her tell his story by teaching catechism to other village children and helping hunted priests escape capture, despite the potential consequences. The Father's response to her trust led her to consecrate her life to God in a secret prayer garden, in the presence of a few family members, friends, and an outlawed priest. She trusted enough to continue sharing and growing in the faith her country was trying to destroy. Her devotion to God and his plan was matched only by her enthusiasm to be a part of his work in a hurting world. Her life as a religious sister was met with great trials and poverty, and for a long time she searched for a place to establish an order to do the work she felt so called to do. She persevered in trust through all the obstacles, including the objection of her earthly father.

On the heels of her faith and trust in the will of the Father, Anne-Marie was led to a rich life of service to the poor, the young, the needy and the outcast. The work of her order took many turns, and her sisters cared for people in situations she could never have imagined, from orphans to the dying to newly released slaves. All the work she and her sisters did was sprinkled with difficulty and opposition.

At one point, the orphanage Anne-Marie had opened ran completely out of food. As she sat in the chapel deep in prayer, she poured out her heart, asking God to punish her if he desired but to please not punish the children. Anne-Marie shared later that she heard the Lord's voice remind her to trust and assured her that he would attend to those he had placed in her care. With a trusting heart she left the chapel to find a wagonload of food being delivered by her own father. Despite his opposition to the life she had chosen, he told her he couldn't very well let her starve. This situation was one of the many times she called on the Lord in trust, and he demonstrated his love. Despite all the obstacles her work faced, before she died, her sisters were working on five continents to educate, evangelize, nurse, and love God's children of all colors, ages, and station in life. Blessed Anne-Marie, we pray for your intercession to help us live a life of unwavering trust.

Blessed Anne-Marie Javouhey, pray for us!

20
Shut Up and Trust

Trust in the Lord, *and do good;*
so you will dwell in the land, and be nourished in safety.
— Psalm 37:3

I had a dream the other night that involved coming face to face with Jesus. It probably stemmed from something I heard on the radio earlier in the day about meeting Jesus and thinking about what you would say to him. So there I was in my cozy bed, and the sweet image of me walking toward Jesus filled my dreamy mind. Instead of my speaking to him the well-crafted words I had practiced in my mind, Jesus looked at me, raised an eyebrow, and spoke first. He simply looked into my eyes and said, "Sheri, just shut up and trust me!" I have to tell you, that dream left me more than a little bit rattled. I had this whole tender, powerful, loving scene cooked up in my head and what I got was a straight, blunt, bottom-line directive delivered with the tact of an older brother instead of a loving Father. The whole scene stuck with me like a license plate for several days, and then it all began to make sense.

A couple of years ago, I heard a great speaker say that upon waking each morning, before our feet even hit the floor, we should pray sincerely the following words: "Lord, I trust you and give you this day; come into my heart and change me, drawing me closer to you." It's great advice, and I do as he suggested daily, but I'm not sure how sincere or expectant I am about it. I offer those words and then think about the ways I want him to change me and draw me near. I often try to make things easy for God and do his work for him. I have a picture in my head of how my life should look and how I will serve and what my blessings will be. I have it all boxed, wrapped, and packaged neatly for God — and going through the motions of that prayer each morning sometimes feels more like a confirmation than an invitation. No wonder Jesus put things in such plain English for me!

That silly dream has caused me to reflect quite a bit! The hardest part of truly trusting the work of the Lord in my life is accepting his plan when it is hugely different than mine.

Blessed Anne-Marie was a model of abandoning expectations. Time after time, she followed where the Lord led — and then things didn't go as planned, and sometimes the work she and her sisters were called to do seemed a complete failure, yet she humbly accepted the next task with trust. You'd think by now I'd realize the Lord does much better work than I could ever imagine doing myself! My mind has been flooded the past several days with examples of how he took over and did really cool stuff when I did as Jesus suggested in my dream ... just shut up and trust! I think one of the biggest surprises has been this book. Before the Lord took over my computer, the only thing I was writing was my grocery list! Who knew? Well ... God did! There have been so many moments during the creation of this book when I had no idea what to write, but each time that happened, I surrendered, trusting the Holy Spirit to send me something folks need to hear. And poof ... you're holding the book! This is completely the work of trusting a loving God, because I have no training or background as a writer. On all my bucket lists, "become a writer" never appeared! It makes me giggle because I think if he can do this with me, what else could he do if we just trusted him?

Trusting in the will of the Father is an amazing thing. We strive to be strong, independent, and self-reliant, but instead God invites us to be completely dependent on him. It isn't weakness but rather a strength far greater than we can muster up ourselves. I keep thinking about that dream and wondering how many other areas of my life I need to "shut up and trust" him with. Perhaps I need to get out my prayer journal and do my own homework assignment today. I hope you will too!

To grow in joyful trust: Make a list of those things in your life that you need to surrender completely to God, trusting faithfully in his will.

Blessed Anne-Marie Javouhey, pray for us!

21
Hold the Invitations

Give thanks in all circumstances; for this is the will of God in Christ Jesus for you. — 1 Thessalonians 5:18

Have you ever had one of those days when you just felt that you wanted to throw yourself a big ol' pity party? You know the days — something goes wrong with the car, the kids, and the job, and someone gets glowing credit for something you did! Those kinds of days happen to us all, and they go down with a big sting. We usually crawl in bed feeling unappreciated, overworked, and guilty for feeling so sorry for ourselves. I call it "getting in touch with your inner toddler." The bad part of this deal is when you let it drag you down and cloud the way you think and act for days. Today, I have just the story that will be the party pooper at your pity party.

There is a woman very dear to me who is one of the most beautiful examples of trust, faith, and strength I know! She is in a battle against the monster we know as cancer. The reports from her army of doctors have been like a rollercoaster. She has been through treatment after treatment, gone into remission with a hope-filled heart only to receive another diagnosis proclaiming the opposite news. She has lost and regrown hair; she has gone from joy to grief to anxiety to hope again and again. Her diagnosis and treatment have changed like a chameleon, but one thing has not changed — her spirit of trust! Sure, she has her bad days and her scary days and her worried days, but you would never really know it because she inspires everyone she knows with her faith, attitude, and trust in the Lord. She is larger than life, and everyone whose life she touches is richer because of her. I wonder sometimes if people like my friend, who fights her battle with humility and trust, touch more lives than we can even fathom. I'm sure she wouldn't have imagined all the ways she's helped people grow toward sainthood. Blessed Anne-Marie shared the same spirit of trust and humility, and despite setbacks and roadblocks, she started an order that serves God's beloved in almost sixty countries. The growth and influence of her service is a shining example of the fancy things the Father can do. She trusted him when the world doubted her, she persevered when people and things blocked her path, and she searched for the open window when the doors seemed to close. When she received something in prayer, she proceeded to put it into action, and when superiors or authorities or lack of funds said no, she faithfully returned to the Father seeking his confirmation and trusting his redirection. God uses all things for his great good even when it doesn't seem like it.

I chatted with my friend at a ball game one night, and it was a mix of laughter, hugs, and faith rooted in trust. She has a spark that makes you feel alive, and every time someone walks away from a conversation with her, they say the same exact thing: "She is amazing!" During our conversation, she mentioned that she was always working on trusting the will of God more. I wanted to say, "Hey, sister, you trust him any more, and he's gonna put you in charge!" Part of what makes her so amazing is that she is so humble; she doesn't even realize how powerful and inspiring her unbridled trust and her strength really are. She's teaching all of us who know her, and, my, what a wonderful, beautiful teacher she is! In my hurting heart I was thinking how unfair all her suffering seemed, but later in prayer God gently reminded me that humans look for and demand what we think is the fair way, instead of praying for the trust to realize there is only his way. His way is outcome-based. His way is the way that leads us to heaven, while our way just leads to a seat at the head table of a pity party.

Some folks say there are no real miracles anymore. I disagree completely! They are right in front of our eyes if we just look a little. If we can stop living in our me-centered world long enough to see the discomfort, strife, pain, and struggles of another, our hearts and our perspectives will be changed.

People like my friend are the antidote to those folks who wake up with a hangnail and think the world is ending. She's the antidote to all those who think money and stuff matter. She is one of the many miracles right before our very eyes that show us exactly what matters. So, before you send out the invitations to your pity party, let me introduce you to my friend — or, better yet, I'll bet you know someone like her too. Take some time to let that person teach you something!

To grow in joyful trust: Make a list of all the things you have to complain about, then reach out to someone who is sick, lonely, or suffering and pray together for the courage to trust the Father.

Blessed Anne-Marie Javouhey, pray for us!

22
Wise Words

But God shows his love for us in that while we were yet sinners Christ died for us. — Romans 5:8

Saint Augustine once gave a sermon in which he proposed a kind of self-test to see if we truly love God. He told the congregation: "Suppose God proposed you a deal and said, 'I will give you anything you want. You can possess the whole world. Nothing will be impossible for you; nothing will be a sin, nothing forbidden. You will never die, never have pain, never have anything you do not want and always have everything you do want … except for one thing: You will never see my face.'" Saint Augustine closed with a question: "Did a chill arise in your hearts when you heard the words "You will never see my face?' That chill is the most precious thing in you; that is the pure love of God and born of that love is trust."

Every time I think about the wise words of this story, I get such a wave of desire — desire to trust more, desire to try harder to be holy, and desire to truly see his face! After listening to a priest talk about Saint Augustine's words, I have a renewed sense of purpose, a new strength, a new hope. I think we work so hard at doing the "right thing" that maybe we forget just what we're working for. It's easy to get into the habit of doing good things so that others will think we're "nice." In the words of a former parish priest, "Nowhere in the Bible are we called to be nice!" We are called to trust, to hope, to be holy, to be uncomfortable, to realize sometimes the Gospels hit us sideways … and that's OK! We are called to do the hard work of following Christ, being his hands and feet on earth — and that, as we all know, isn't always easy. There are days when that offer from God that Saint Augustine talked about seems like a great idea! Those are the times we need to set out with new energy to grow in trust and to do his work, knowing it won't be without great blessing and reward.

The great reward of heaven is to see the face of God. During those seasons when we wonder if it's worth all the work to get there, we can turn to the Father in prayer. I was wondering about all of this while my sixth graders were making inspirational posters for All Saints' Day. One of the kids made a poster with a quote she had found from St. Jane Frances de Chantal. In lovely cursive, this young lady copied the words "Hold your eyes on God and leave the doing to him. That is all the doing you have to worry about." It's easy to look at our world right now, find the bad, and get caught in the crazy. Without too much effort, we might even think things are worse now than they've ever been, but Saint Jane Frances lived and probably wrote these words to encourage believers in her time when they believed they were in the middle of the worst times. I suppose it's all relative! The truth isn't really in the circumstances; the truth is in the Father. No matter how sidetracked or fuzzy-headed or overwhelmed we feel, we have to hold our eyes on him and let him do the doing! And his "doing" is pretty amazing!

Our number one task is to get to heaven. It's what we were made for. Everything we do, say, listen to, or watch, and everyone we hang out with, will either help us get there or draw us away. We weren't made to live in isolation. We were created to work, pray, and play together and to help each other grow in holiness so that we will all someday see the face of God. Blessed Anne-Marie often reminded her sisters that nothing was done on their own; God guided them to work and serve and love as a community because that was a powerful force. The temptation is there to think one little thing or one little relationship or one little bad habit here or there won't matter — but it's still a step away from our purpose. The most powerful thing I can think of to make those decisions easier is to remember what's waiting for us in heaven: the face of God. I also realize that the business of getting to heaven to see his face is business that begins today, not next week or next Lent. Blessed Anne-Marie realized this, too, and encouraged those she served and served with to be in the present when she shared the words, "We must be of our time in order to win it for Christ!" That's something worth trusting, worth fighting for, worth being hopeful about.

To grow in joyful trust: Print the words to Saint Augustine's sermon and read them every day this week. I'm willing to bet if you let these wise words really sink into your heart, living the gospel message will have a new meaning!

Blessed Anne-Marie Javouhey, pray for us!

23
Slingshot Shootin'

So David prevailed over the Philistine with a sling and with a stone. — 1 Samuel 17:50

Hands down, the story of David and Goliath is an Old Testament favorite among the little lovelies every year. I reread it for about the tenth time not long ago, and the slingshot seemed to stay in my mind. It's really a crazy story when you think about it. Since I can't hit the refrigerator with a rubber band, you can probably breathe easy if I approach you with a slingshot — odds are good my shot won't be within five feet of my target. It was such an odd weapon of choice for David, don't you think? I wonder what the giant must have thought as this very young soldier stood before him with it ... did he find it insulting or funny or insanely ridiculous? I wonder if it made him angry, or if he just wanted to bust out laughing.

Lately I seem to be confronting the "giants" in my day with a slingshot. Although David was able to conquer with it, I'm afraid I'm not so successful. I seem to keep missing the target, and I wonder what God must think as he watches me wildly fling stones around and not really conquer the things that creep between us. I'm sure on some occasions he must have a good laugh at me; I must look like a nut throwing sand at an approaching army.

I do believe that I often miss the whole point of the David and Goliath story. It wasn't about David and his slingshot at all. It was about the power of God working through an open, trusting, and expectant heart. David didn't doubt; he just knew God would conquer. The truth is that David could have faced that enemy with a paper clip or a cotton ball and defeated Goliath, because it was the power of God that did the work, not the power of man.

I'm not so good at living with the trust found in that part of the story. It's not about the size of the battle or the weapon; it's the size of the faith and trust that determines the outcome. Where God wills a battle to be won in a mighty way, he shows up and amazes us.

Blessed Anne-Marie and her sisters were sent to prepare a large group of slaves for emancipation. Their work and training and ministry were bearing amazing fruit, sparking jealousy, and a plot was hatched for the canoe guide to tip the boat and launch Blessed Anne-Marie into alligator-infested waters, ensuring her demise. When it came down to it, the boat guide was overcome by the Lord and could not bring himself to do what he'd been ordered to do. God is mighty, and his plans will triumph every time!

When we become people of trust, God can do mighty things to and through us, things we don't even see coming. My friend told an amazing story not long ago about trust. The story came at the perfect time because my "trust tank" was running a little low, making me the opposite of David.

The story was about a man who had been shipwrecked but by the grace of God was able to salvage supplies for his survival. He was so grateful for God's goodness, and he thanked him because even though this terrible thing had happened, God provided the supplies and a way to save them. The man built a hut to house and protect the supplies essential for his survival and again offered his praise and thanksgiving to the Father. Then disaster struck again, and the hut that contained the lifesaving goods burned to the ground. In fear, hopelessness, and desperation, he cried out to God and asked why he had abandoned him and allowed him to suffer such a debilitating loss. As he contemplated his certain demise, he spotted a ship that had come to his rescue. The captain of the ship told him what a brilliant idea it had been to build such a huge fire to signal help. He told the man that the ship had been headed in a completely different direction, but seeing such a huge amount of smoke, the captain realized it clearly must have been someone signaling for help, so he immediately changed course and came to his rescue.

If there are hiccups and speed bumps in my life, it isn't because God messed up or forgot about me; it's because he's getting me ready for the next thing. Since I can't possibly know what that next thing is, I probably shouldn't waste my time building a hut to protect the stuff I think I need to get there. I can't possibly know, so I shouldn't pack, store, and prepare … I simply need to trust, obey, and stick to his plan. He's already shown me patience, love, grace, mercy, and blessings beyond imagination and proved he is faithful and trustworthy. I need the trust of David.

To grow in joyful trust: Read the story of David and Goliath. Seriously contemplate the things you're trying to slay with a slingshot, and then figure out which ones you need to hand over to God's precise aim.

Blessed Anne-Marie Javouhey, pray for us!

24
Trust the Master Planner

A man's mind plans his way,
but the Lord directs his steps. — Proverbs 16:9

A recent week looked as though it would be one crazy mess. There was not one day when I had more than an hour at a time without something scheduled. After my lovely, peaceful, quiet, slow-paced summer, that week felt as if I had been tangled up in a tornado. I remember looking at my schedule and thinking I might hyperventilate or croak. Well, I'm happy to report that not only did I survive, but it was a terrific week! You want to know why? I gave the week completely to God.

Sometimes I get a little sassy with God. On that Monday morning, I told him we had a serious problem that I couldn't manage. I told him I needed help. As I sat in quiet prayer, the words that came to my mind were "Thank you for the invitation, Sheri, but I don't need your help at all; just trust me and give the week completely and totally to me." Of course, I argued with him a little, and in my sassiness, I reminded him that the week included finishing my classroom, an all-day meeting, an all-day volleyball tournament, overnight company, a parent conference, cleaning the house and garage to host a party for a few dozen guests, a prayer meeting, a book club meeting, an eye exam, a family wedding, and several other events sprinkled in just for fun! I can't even explain the feeling of complete peace that washed over me and blanketed me as I lifted it all up to him. Blessed Anne-Marie knew this peace. She was often heard repeating, "I am in God's hands, ready to do God's will as soon as it is revealed to me." To her they weren't just words; they were her guide and the source of her delight and consolation.

Here are some of the highlights. Two high school students showed up one morning out of nowhere to help me work in my classroom. The all-day meeting was great nourishment for my soul. The volleyball tournament was one laugh after another with some really great parents. The eye appointment that was supposed to take more than an hour was done in twenty-five minutes. Band practice was canceled the night we had an overnight guest, so I had extra help from Shannon with dinner and entertaining. The overnight company was so much fun and filled the time with laughter, prayer, and excellent conversation. The prayer and book club meetings were full of blessings. Some car trouble made it necessary to change the location of the prayer meeting to our house. I got home and had an hour to get the house tidied and bake a dessert. I decided to make chocolate chip bar cookies and discovered that nearly the entire bag of chocolate chips had been eaten, but then I spied a bag of forgotten M&M's in the back of the pantry! I stood in awe as one thing after another just clicked perfectly into place. There was not one minute of struggle or stress the entire week. He even took care of a major wardrobe malfunction. As I was getting ready for the wedding, the zipper in my dress wouldn't do its job and close the back of my dress … not a good look! As I jammed it back into the closet and searched for something to wear, a hanger fell to the floor containing a skirt that I hadn't even considered. As I bent to pick it up, I hit my head on the shelf and off tumbled a top that I had never worn with that skirt. I had the perfect necklace lying on the dresser, so I was ready in a flash in what seemed like a totally new outfit. We got home from the volleyball tournament more than an hour before the party guests arrived, and the weather was perfect, and the laughter and friendship were great.

He took it all!

I have to let you in on a little secret, though. My part of the deal was to make sure that no matter how busy the day was, I had to trust him completely and make sure I didn't cheat him out of any of his minutes during morning prayer. One morning when I was tempted to cut it short to get moving a little sooner, the person I was supposed to meet with called and said she would be running about thirty minutes late. God even made sure we had time to be together. I believe that when we trust him, God multiplies time — and I've never felt so loved!

To grow in joyful trust: Hand over with great trust your schedule and your to-do list … really give it to him and be prepared to be loved and amazed!

Blessed Anne-Marie Javouhey, pray for us!

25
Waiting with Trust

The Lord is good to those who wait for him,
to the soul that seeks him. — Lamentations 3:25

If you were to give yourself a score between one and ten (ten being awesome), how would you score yourself at waiting? Are you patient, still, and peaceful as you wait, or are you fidgety, anxious, and impatient? What would you think if I told you I was going to give you a free trip to sit in a waiting room? I'm not sure how many would find that much of a trip at all — but maybe it could be if we took a different look at waiting and the things that can happen to us while we trust the Lord to be present in our waiting.

One December many years ago, I was sitting in the waiting rooms at Mayo Clinic with Mom for an entire week. Each year when I put up our Nativity set, I am reminded of a simple blessing of all that waiting. As we waited and waited, I began to visit with people who were also waiting and met a lovely couple from Wisconsin who made the waiting so much better. They radiated trust, faith, and peace even in their suffering and fear. Throughout the week he would whittle little pieces of wood, and she would card wool from the sheep they raised. On the last day we were at the clinic, they told Dad and me they would be praying for us, and they handed each of us a set of Nativity animals made from the wood he had carved and whittled and the wool she had carded. Each year as I unpack that set, I pray for that couple and remember the gift of their talent and their friendship and prayers during a time of frustrated waiting. They were our Mayo Clinic blessing, a blessing God's grace brought in our waiting. They shifted our thoughts from our heartache and worries to the joy of the season we were preparing for. I later realized they were the introduction to an important lesson in waiting with trust. They helped me begin to understand that there is a big difference between waiting for God to do what I want and waiting with God as he unfolds his perfect will. The second requires loving trust.

I think we're all waiting for something. What are you waiting for? Maybe you're waiting for a new job or a headache to go away. Perhaps your wait is more serious, like waiting for a baby, for test results, for a lost love to return, or for a diagnosis. Perhaps you're waiting for someone to get car keys so that you don't have so much carpooling to do, or for a little one to finally sleep through the night or master the art of potty training. Many are waiting for a blanket of sadness, grief, or loneliness to be lifted from their heavy heart. We spend months just waiting for something to start or something to stop so something else can start. The honest truth is that many of us are simply waiting on God to organize our life just the way we've been planning it, just waiting for him to do his job the way we'd like it, instead of trusting in him.

Since we spend so much time waiting, the kind of wait-er we are matters. Blessed Anne-Marie had her share of patient waiting. Several times as she served the poor, needy, and sick, she herself contracted illness and afflictions that took her out of service. She learned to make these times of deep prayer and offered her sacrifice for the work of her sisters.

The prophet Isaiah promised that those who wait for the Lord will have their strength renewed. I could use a little of that! The fruit of waiting patiently is peace. That peace gives way to trust, humility, and docility. What if we invited God into our waiting? What if we offered him the seat right next to us? Through that attitude of humility and docility that comes with peace, we might begin to realize that the job we've been waiting for might not be ours at all; maybe it's the perfect job for someone else. What if that person we've been waiting to love us is meant to love somebody else because God has someone chosen who will love us far more than the person we had in mind ever could? What if healing meant making our soul healthier than our body so that we could enjoy eternity with Jesus instead of spending more years on earth? What if we became so full of trust and so good at waiting that we grew in humility to such a point we rejoiced when others got something and forgot we were even waiting in the first place? What if we realized all the waiting we do has a great purpose, one we usually can't see? Not to worry, God can see it. Someday we'll figure it out and realize that when we patiently wait for him to bring everything to complete perfection, we are blessed with something so much better than we even hoped for!

Worrying and waiting is exhausting; everybody knows that. Well, here's a newsflash — waiting is supposed to be an inactive thing, so we shouldn't be worn out. If we are waiting right, we trust and we are in peace, letting time pass with contentment, knowing God has it all under control. Instead, we get worn out because we fight and squirm and wrestle with God's plan, just sure that he's forgotten or misunderstood our needs. When I get like that, I hear my mother's voice say, "Now, Sheri Ann, just settle down, miss, settle down and trust the one who loves you most!" Good advice as always.

To grow in joyful trust: What are you waiting for? Make a list, and with trust in your heart ask God to take your worries and waiting and exchange them for peace and patience.

Blessed Anne-Marie Javouhey, pray for us!

26
Trust and Hope

But they who wait for the Lord *shall renew their strength,*
they shall mount up with wings like eagles,
they shall run and not be weary,
they shall walk and not faint. — *Isaiah 40:31*

H*ope* is a word I misuse all the time. I say things like "I hope it doesn't rain," or "I hope there is a parking spot close to the door." When I really think about it, the things I "hope" for are usually things that would make my life convenient or pleasant. Lately I have been challenged to look at the way I use the word *hope*. The first thing I needed to do was compare the worldly definition (the one I most often used) to the virtue of hope. Here's what I found. Hope is commonly used to refer to a wish connected to a person's desire. But godly hope, the virtue of hope, is the confident expectation of what God has promised, and its strength is in his faithfulness. Hope, used the proper way, means I need to see things bigger — and that requires trust.

I love it when God teaches a lesson through real people! One week I met a beautiful woman who told me she was a woman of trust and hope. She shared that for years she had prayed that her family would grow closer. Her children were grown and had moved away, and she longed for them to be more connected and involved in each other's life. She said she always trusted that God could do that, but it wasn't until recently that she began to see him work. She said the things God was doing in her family were filling her with such abundant hope. As I listened to her share her story, my heart both sunk and swelled as she told me that she was dying of cancer, but she was so filled with hope because God had used this situation to answer her prayer. Fighting the disease had been the thing that drew her family together. She told me she was not afraid to die but rather filled with hope, because God had answered her prayer and brought her family so close together. She knew they would support each other and care for her husband and make sure he didn't get too lonely when she was gone. I was in awe as I hugged this beautiful soul and took in a lesson on the true meaning of the words *trust* and *hope.*

God used another event to thump me with the word *hope* by demonstrating his faithfulness in a mighty way in the lives of an incredible newlywed couple. As I took my spot in the church for this beautiful wedding, my heart was a little on the heavy side. The groom had lost both of his parents in a car crash just about a year before, and as I sat in the pew waiting for Mass to begin, I wondered if he and his bride would feel the same joy as other couples do on their wedding day. I wondered what Father Eric could say to honor the event, the couple, and the parents of the groom. Just when my tears were about to get out of control, I remembered that God is bigger than our pain and that he loved that bride and groom more than they loved each other. When it came time for the homily, the hope came barging in! Father spoke of the new life of Easter and the new life of marriage. He also talked about the beginnings and the scars that bring us to the important events in our lives. I watched this beautiful new couple laugh and smile, and I watched their family and closest friends cling to the laughter and joy of the day, and I realized the only way that all happened was because of hope. They trusted in the Father's love, and it brought the hope that joy would follow pain. They trusted the truth that God will never leave us stuck in our scars and our pain. Their trust brought the hope that he has a plan and that he works in every situation, not just the fancy, happy, simple ones.

The Lord reveals his plan and creates opportunities for us to hope and trust constantly. Sometimes they are easy to miss, like a subtle thought running through our mind, but every once in a while, he uses bold, unmistakable signs to draw us nearer to his plan. Blessed Anne-Marie once experienced a vision of St. Teresa of Avila entrusting children of all different races to her. St. Teresa of Avila was a great inspiration and model of faithfulness to Blessed Anne-Marie, so this vision was a loving invitation from a spiritual friend to think bigger and trust harder. God showed her not just one kind of child from one geographic location but an array of needs and races and places that would need her love and her service. The more we ask for the Lord to help us grow in trust, the clearer things become, because trust is a fruit of love. The more we love the Father, the more we trust him. Hope born of trust is understanding that God has promised good for his children and that good rises from the ashes of awful. I saw hope rise on that wedding day, and it was so much bigger than the sadness.

To grow in joyful trust: With a heart filled with trust, make a list of things you hope for.

Blessed Anne-Marie Javouhey, pray for us!

27
Trust Is Tricky

Trust in the Lord with all your heart,
and do not rely on your own insight. — Proverbs 3:5

Trust can be a tricky thing. We live in a world that promotes independence and self-sufficiency, but we follow a God who promotes the opposite. The world says, "Grab it! Take charge of it! Look out for yourself! Be great!" The Father who created us and adores us says, "Let go. I have the plan. Surrender to me, and I will lead you to a life far more magnificent than you can fathom!" On paper the decision seems pretty simple, but trusting him can be tough. We're conditioned to muscle our way through, but he wants to fight for us, so each day needs to be an exercise in letting him.

Blessed Anne-Marie loved and served and obeyed with determination. Her determination was not about getting her way, though — it was about helping others trust the Father's plan as much as she did. Working for the good of the Lord and his people is tough work sometimes, and Anne-Marie was referred to as a "velvet brick." She had a "layer of gentleness covering her determined core." Her service to the Lord was always rooted in humility and her prayerful attempts to do the Father's work.

God and I have an agreement about my travel. I ask him to

get me where I need to be on time because people and schedules are counting on me, but I promise to let him do anything he wants with my trip home, without complaint. I offer any struggle or inconvenience that I might want to whine about for the people I just worked with and the people I love or who need prayers. I started this deal with the Father for two reasons. First, I know we can never get to heaven without some suffering, and second, there are so many people who need prayer, so offering up any of my inconvenience is a prayerful gift. But there is also a third reason: It helps me grow in trust. And, of course, I just get a kick out of seeing how fancy he is and how he shows his love and care for me when I do actually trust him. He's done some pretty funny stuff on my trips home, but one weekend he showed his fanciness in a giant way.

As usual, I got to Oklahoma City with travel that was smooth as silk! It was a spectacular weekend, and I met some truly amazing, faith-filled people of all ages. The hospitality and friendly conversation absolutely filled my heart. I got up at three in the morning on Sunday to begin my journey home. I had a 3:45 a.m. Uber to get me to the airport for a very early flight. As I got in the elevator on the fourteenth floor, I wasn't expecting any other passengers, but the elevator stopped on floor thirteen, and two folks joined me. As soon as the door closed, the elevator took off like a rocket and stopped with a slam between floors six and seven. The first thing I thought was "We're OK … thank you, Jesus!" The lady was struggling in a big way, and as I was praying in my head and feeling complete peace, it occurred to me that I should pray out loud so that the young couple could feel it too … and they did. The second thing I thought was, "Oh no, the Uber is gonna leave because I'll be late." I just smiled to myself knowing God would find me a later flight. A short time later, two firemen arrived, pried open the doors, and lifted us out. When I got to the lobby, I rushed out the hotel door, only to discover that the fire truck was blocking the Uber driver, so he had to wait for me. My TSA PreCheck status number had arrived the day before I left on that trip, so I was able to zip through security and make my flight. I buckled up thinking how many times God just takes care of every little thing. The TSA number wasn't supposed to arrive for another month, but he knew I'd need it earlier; nobody was hurt in the elevator; the firemen arrived quickly; the young couple yelled from across the hotel lobby as I got in the Uber, "Thank you for praying; we should start doing that!" He is always right there, and when my eyes are on him with trust, I see what he's doing along the way. The only thing I might have to complain about is that my flight was so early Starbucks wasn't even open!

Following the wise advice of Mother Teresa, we should remember to pray for trust instead of clarity. Surrendering my travel is such a simple way to trust more, plus it's just plain funny to see all the ways he works. When we were getting ready to land in Atlanta, the pilot announced that we would need to circle the airport again because the landing flap wasn't working properly. I decided to use those twenty minutes to pray a Rosary for everyone who is sick and struggling. We touched down perfectly just as I finished the last prayer. He's just so fancy! I'm not sure who needed that Rosary at that specific time, but I know I wouldn't have prayed it if we hadn't heard that announcement. I trust he did something lovely with those prayers. I never get home on time or when my ticket says I will, but it sure makes for great stories and gives me lots of chances to trust him and see where he's working in my life.

To grow in joyful trust: What can you surrender to the Lord that might help you grow in trust?

Blessed Anne-Marie Javouhey, pray for us!

The Fourth Gift

Joyful Prayer

28
St. Francis de Sales

Those who pray from the heart do not think about the prayer they are saying, but about the God to whom they pray. — St. Francis de Sales

As adults, there are dozens of things we do every day out of habit with little or no thought at all. We don't need an instruction manual to brush our teeth or tie our shoes; we don't need a yellow sticky note on the door reminding us to change out of our PJs before we go to work. These are just a part of the natural flow of the day. I don't recall ever needing to write someone a note with instructions on how to breathe; we just do it. Can we say the same about our prayer life? Is it an absolutely fundamental part of each and every day without fail, instruction, or hesitation? Prayer is the root from which our holiness and sainthood grow, but we often settle for slipping it in wherever it fits.

Since joy is best defined as being in the will of God, the way we see his will revealed to us is in prayer. Prayer is how we communicate with the Father, so in the daily prayerful dialogue with him, we are directed, corrected, strengthened, and guarded. Prayer connects us to the giver of life, allows us to recognize his presence, and creates in us a spirit of great joy!

St. Francis de Sales relied on the strength and grace found in a life lived deeply rooted in prayer. After he was ordained a priest, he was sent to an area in Switzerland that was very hostile to Catholics. He was persecuted, excluded, and viewed by many as an outcast, pushed away for his message. He spent much of his time living outside or in barns even in the cold of winter. His ministry left him cold, hungry, and unsuccessful by worldly standards — but his fervent prayer life sustained him and led him to find another way. Since people were not favorable to listening to him when he tried to spread the Good News of Jesus, he took to writing little pamphlets about prayer and the love of the Lord and slipping them under people's doors. Guided by prayer, his quiet way of reaching souls actually led to the conversion of more than forty thousand people.

St. Francis de Sales is a Doctor of the Church whose writings are filled with wisdom and glorious truth. Through his brilliant mind, works of spiritual genius written centuries ago guide us yet today. His writings have helped form the minds of the learned and the simple because in his work are simple truths intended to reach the hearts of the faithful. He believed prayer and holiness to be the mission of everyone in all stations of life. In response to the directive in Paul's First Letter to the Thessalonians to "pray constantly" (5:17), he proposed the simple prayer "ask, offer, accept." In every situation we ask God to be present with us and to make us aware of his promptings. Every situation we offer for the glory of God, and every situation we lift in prayer and accept whatever comes. We can offer this prayer dozens of times a day for things that are hard, confusing, and joyful. Our asking becomes a channel of grace, our offering becomes our sacrifice, and our acceptance allows us to trust and grow in faith.

Prayer is not a box we check off daily; it is a way of life … an integral and pivotal part of our day. St. Francis de Sales taught that the Lord wants the first fruits of our day, and he often counseled those who came to seek his wisdom that every Christian needs a half hour of prayer a day, except when he's busy — and then he needs an hour. St. Francis de Sales, we pray for your intercession to help us become people of deep prayer.

St. Francis de Sales, pray for us!

29
Seeking

Speak, Lord, for your servant hears. — 1 Samuel 3:9

When I was growing up, if I misplaced something and said, "I can't find it!" my dad would always say, "I'm sure it will be in the last place you look." He was right; it always was — but as a kid that line really bugged me! I think it probably bugged me because what I would have rather heard him say was, "I'll help you find it." That simple statement of the obvious, and the reality that I was on my own, was his very simple way of letting me know that I was responsible. If I wanted that missing object badly enough, I had to invest the thought, energy, and action into finding what I was looking for.

Not long ago, I heard someone say, "God just never listens to me!" I'm sure we've all felt that way a time or two when things got bumpy, but the question that should always follow that statement is "How well do I listen to God?" As Christians we can be assured of God's presence in our lives. But sometimes, we have to do what my dad always pushed me to do: take responsibility for finding his loving presence in our lives. God speaks to us, but it's not a bold, booming, deep voice from the clouds. God speaks to us daily if we're seeking and listening. There are four ways he makes us aware of his presence, his voice, and his will.

The first way God speaks to us is through Scripture. Once while I was in the middle of a struggle, I tried a dozen things on my own to make it better. Finally, after no improvement, I did what I should have done first: I went to God's word for strength, comfort, and counsel. When I did finally ask God to speak to my heart, I landed on James 1:2–3: "Count it all joy, my brethren, when you meet various trials, for you know that the testing of your faith produces steadfastness." I heard that loud and clear!

The second way God speaks to us is through circumstances. Sometimes we call them coincidences, but God deserves the credit for those things, not fate. God so loves each of us that he arranges and organizes events and circumstances all the time just to show us how much he loves us and cares for us. Keep your eye out for them!

The third way is through people. Sometimes the right person with just the right word comes along at just right time, and it seems to change everything. That's God, speaking through others. A lady shared a story just recently about being in the hospital. As she was being prepped for surgery, a nurse walked in to assist, and they just "out of nowhere" started talking about trusting God and feeling his peace. She said it completely removed her fear, and she rolled down the hall with an amazing sense of calmness and confidence.

The fourth way God speaks to us is through prayer. My husband and I can't raise our children together if we don't talk. I can't teach a room full of little lovelies to read or do math if we don't talk. I think we understand that we would stumble around in such chaos and frustration if we didn't communicate with each other. Prayer is our communication with God. It's the most important conversation we have each day — yet it's the one that gets pushed to the side when we get busy or frazzled.

There are two big mistakes we can make when mapping out

our prayer time. The first is to think we don't have time to pray. Saying we don't have time to pray is like trying to drive somewhere and saying we're so busy we don't have time to put gas in the car. The second mistake is thinking prayer is important only if our plan needs back up. Prayer is what allows God to reveal his plan, which is always superior to our plan or our wishes and expectations. St. Francis de Sales's wise words remind us that "Prayer … is so useful and necessary that without it we could not come to any good, seeing that by means of prayer we are shown how to perform all our actions well."

If you feel that something's missing in your life, seek the giver of all good things. He might be in the last place you look, but he'll be there waiting.

To grow in joyful prayerfulness: Pick one of the four ways and start seeking him. I'm willing to bet that the more you seek him in these four places, the more you'll find him.

St. Francis de Sales, pray for us!

30
Praying Together

For where two or three are gathered in my name, there am I in the midst of them. — *Matthew 18:20*

Every now and again I hear something that just grabs me right by the eardrums. Recently, I heard a priest giving a reflection focused on our personal need for more prayer, and he made some excellent points and had some great stories. He was a dynamic speaker, so I was pretty tuned in, but then he said something that made my jaw drop. He said, "People are sleeping together before they are praying together!" He went on to say that praying with another person is such an intimate thing to do that many people find it too uncomfortable. My head just couldn't let go of that thought! After I had puddled around with that idea for a few weeks, another one came to mind — if prayer was what people in a relationship did first, how would that change the relationship? And even more importantly, how would it change the culture?

As a wife and mother, I am constantly examining the way I fulfill my roles. More often than not, I'm asking for forgiveness for not getting things right with my husband and my kids. In my search to do my job better, I often watch and listen to women I respect. I like to know how others do it well. I like to talk to moms and dads who have raised great kids and couples who have beautiful loving marriages. I want to know how to get it right! In all my conversations I have made an important discovery. The folks who seem to "get it right" are the ones who are people of prayer. Christ is at the center of their marriage, their friendships, and their parenting, and, boy, can you see the difference that makes.

I saw a billboard once that said, "Prayer changes everything!" I suppose that is a completely true and powerful statement. If any of us have complained about the decline in the morals and ethics of our society, I think it's fair to say we know the antidote: prayer. St. Francis de Sales said, "[Prayer] is the water of blessing which by its watering causes the plants of our good desires to become green and to flower, washes our souls clean from their imperfections, and quenches the passions of our hearts."

Many of you reading this are great prayer warriors. We are great at praying for others in need, but how are we at praying with others? If it's about as comfortable for you as burlap underwear, then there is only one thing to do about that — practice! I'm not asking you to stand on the corner and pray out loud for an hour; I'm asking you to find one person and ask him the most powerful question ever: "How can I pray for you?" If we pray with others, we can become a person of prayer, and, boy, could the world use more of those. If someone you know is having a rough day, ask her if she would like to pray for a minute. You can pray together a familiar prayer, like the Lord's Prayer, or maybe share a Scripture verse; or it can be as simple as "Lord, please bless my friend who is struggling today." The power of that simple act is overwhelming!

When people see the power of prayer in action, they feel the invitation to become people of prayer themselves, and that prayer has a ripple effect. We have no problem playing cards or games together, sharing stories about the people we work with, or discussing our favorite sport or recipe until we're blue in the face — but none of those things have the potential to redirect a life toward Christ as sharing prayer does. If we want the morals and behavior of a culture to shift, we have to start the shift ourselves, one shared prayer at a time.

To grow in joyful prayerfulness: Pick one person to pray with this week. For extra credit, make it someone you are really close to. Even if he or she declines the invitation, something powerful has been offered.

St. Francis de Sales, pray for us!

31
Prayer Giants

Jesus said to them, "Truly, truly, I say to you, the Son can do nothing of his own accord, but only what he sees the Father doing; for whatever he does, that the Son does likewise." — John 5:19

I find genetics absolutely amazing! Parent–teacher conference night is one of my favorite events of the school year because I love seeing how the kids resemble or imitate their parents. It's fascinating to see how things just seem to run in the family. Sometimes academic or athletic ability seeps into each new generation. The same can be said for musical, theatrical, or artistic talents too.

Not long ago I heard someone talking about "prayer giants." The report pointed out that many families had someone from each generation who just seemed to hold the whole family together like glue with their constant prayers. It made me wonder if praying could be genetic too. After several days of careful thought, I decided becoming a prayer giant is about more than genetics or birth order. I don't think prayerfulness is inherited, like a great jump shot or speedy feet; I think it's learned or developed by following a great example. Who is the prayer giant in your family? If I were a bettin' woman, I would be willing to bet you called to mind someone older than you. I'll admit, so did I at first … but then I gave it some more thought, and I came up with a different idea.

What if there were more than one prayer giant in the family? What if a prayer giant was little? Then I really began thinking about what makes someone a prayer giant. I had a little boy in my class one year who would get more absorbed and lost in prayer than most adults. That same year I had two little lovelies who were always the last to get ready for recess; they would often ask before going out if I'd like them to say a prayer they knew. It isn't just little kids either. I had the privilege of hauling a small group of teenage girls somewhere, and they spent the entire trip discussing the ways God was working in their lives and praying together. I attended a healing prayer service recently, and I was amazed at the number of children and teenagers enthusiastic about being prayed over.

Children are powerful prayer giants, and we often underestimate them. When St. Francis de Sales was trying to spread the message and restore the Catholic Church, people would turn away from his truth, so he turned to the children to teach and share. Soon the parents took notice of the kindness and playfulness and respect shown to their children. It was the children speaking to their parents that led them to seek out the young priest to hear his message. Those children were the path to the Father's truth and love.

We have a new pastor in our parish who has a prayerfulness and faith about him that changes people. I had a visit with the beautiful grandmother of one of my little lovelies recently, and as she hugged and thanked me, she prayed over me as comfortably as if she were reporting on the day's weather. The speaker talking about prayer giants made it seem as though each family has just one prayer giant, but what if each family had more? Wouldn't that make a difference! What if, instead of trying to figure out who the prayer giant in your family is, you decided to become the prayer giant? That would leave a mark on the world for sure!

Our first response to anything should be prayer ... prayer in times of thankfulness, prayer in times of sorrow, prayers in times of celebration, prayer in times of sickness and health. What if we demonstrated to everyone we love that prayer is where we always begin, and everything that happens after will be better? Wouldn't it be amazing if we helped create and inspire so many prayer giants that they outnumbered everyone else in the family? An Orthodox monk known as Elder Thaddeus of Vitovnica said: "It is of great significance if there is a person who truly prays in a family. Prayer attracts God's grace and all the members of the family feel it, even those whose hearts have grown cold. Pray always." If your family could use that kind of grace, keep reading.

How do you become a prayer giant? Here's a good place to start:

1. Set aside the first ten minutes of the day to speak with God, ask for his guidance, and invite him into your heart and your day.
2. Make a list of everyone who needs prayer or blessing and put it in your pocket.
3. Throughout the day, make sure you are praying for people more than you're talking about people.
4. Every time you are compelled to complain about anything, say a prayer for one of the people on your list instead.
5. Pray for each person in your family by name every day.
6. End your day by thanking God for every blessing of the day, followed by an apology for all the places you fell a little short.

Even giants start out small. If we all begin here, we just might make prayerfulness genetic!

To grow in joyful prayerfulness: Begin the six steps for becoming a prayer giant *today*!

St. Francis de Sales, pray for us!

32
But God

Teach me to do your will,
for you are my God!
Let your good spirit lead me
on a level path! — Psalm 143:10

I was standing in the check-out line in the grocery store the other day behind a mom and her five-year-old daughter. As the mother of grown children, it was very easy for me to giggle at the conversation I was hearing because I have so been there, done that, but I could also really sympathize with the mom. The daughter was a negotiator whose favorite phrase was "But Mom!" If I had a dollar for each time that little girl said those words, I could have paid for half my groceries! I was very impressed with the mother's patience and creativity. The little girl wanted — no, needed — a variety of important things that afternoon, like gum, a doll, breath mints, a dart gun, and, of course, sparkly shoes. She carefully outlined all the reasons her needs were valid, and each time mom would counter with logic, she would say, "But Mom," and then go on with three or four ideas to counter the wisdom of her mother. As I stood there laughing to myself, I wondered if that's how I sometimes sound to God.

The truth of the matter is that we argue with God much as that little girl argued with her mom. We try to come up with all kinds of rationale to convince him that our way is right and that there are things we really need. We want to hold tight to the reins, but as St. Francis de Sales told his spiritual friend asking for his action in a situation, "I have to wait to fully know what God wants." I wish I had the spiritual muscle for that kind of patient waiting on the Lord, but, honestly, here is how I see my conversations with God going down most days.

But God … I want to win the lottery; I'd use the money for lots of good things. No, child, I've given you enough.

But God … I should have gotten that; I've worked really hard. No, child, that belonged to one of my other children. Be patient, I have amazing things in store for you.

But God … I'm too busy to sit still and pray for thirty minutes; I've got so many things to do. I mean, after all, I am using the gifts and talents you gave me; isn't that good enough? No, child, I want you to put me first and give me the first fruits of your day so that I can show you what I have planned. Believe me, it will be more productive and enjoyable and blessed than anything you could put on your to-do list.

But God … I pray all the time, in the car, in the shower, in traffic; don't you think that's enough? No, child, I want your full attention so that I can speak to you in the silence and watch your heart become more connected to mine.

But God … can't you take away this suffering? It's just too hard. I thought you loved me. No, child, you are mistaken — suffering doesn't mean I don't love you; it means I'm strengthening you and refining you. You simply need to trust me more so that I can lead you through this (and, by the way, it will bring you so much closer to me than you were before).

But God … you need to stop making life so hard for me. I try to live a good life, but I just keep seeing one disappointment after another while others get everything handed to them and have things so easy. No, child, each of my children has a different path to heaven. Stop comparing, and know everything is perfectly designed to strengthen, purify, and refine you so that you can follow your own path to me. Besides, sweet child, you can only see with your eyes what's on the surface; you have no idea what someone else's path is like. Only I know that.

But God … don't you see what they're doing? It's not fair that I follow the rules while other people do whatever they want, and good things keep happening to them. Maybe I should stop worrying so much about doing everything right and just live however I want. No, child, if you love me, you will follow my commands. And please don't judge others; that's my job, and it's only making your heart dark and snatching away the joy I want you to share.

But God … I want peace, mercy, kindness, and goodness in this world. Good, my child, then love me, trust me, and pray for those things every day, and let me take it from there. You need to slow down, share my love, and let the joy that comes from our friendship spill out everywhere … that's how you get everything you want. Now just be quiet, child, and let me take perfect care of you; I've been doing this job since the beginning of time, and I'm pretty good at it!

To grow in joyful prayerfulness: Make a list of all the things you argue with God about and let him speak to them in the quiet of your prayer time. He's a skilled negotiator!

St. Francis de Sales, pray for us!

33
A Good Trade

O give thanks to the Lord, for he is good;
for his mercy endures for ever! — 1 Chronicles 16:34

Did you ever trade something from your lunchbox when you were a kid? I remember trying to trade tuna salad on Fridays, but it never worked. Apples and oranges never seemed to give me much negotiation power either. I do remember the day I made the trade of the decade. On that memorable day, Mom put two fresh chocolate chip cookies in my lunch, and I was able to trade them for a Twinkie! I was so thrilled, and I couldn't believe the kid fell for those homemade cookies while I walked away with that little package of golden deliciousness. I'd never had a Twinkie, but they were store bought, something we didn't have at our house — so I was sure they must be amazing! I took a bite, and I was instantly disappointed, but I didn't let on. As the afternoon wore on, I learned a valuable lesson about assuming things were better just because they looked fancy, expensive, and well-presented. That was the last time I ever made a lunch trade, and I never told my mom what I'd done because I thought it would hurt her feelings. I also learned that day that something homemade by hands that love you trumps everything, so be very careful about the value of what you're trading!

Since the disappointing Twinkie trade of the '70s, I've become a much more skilled trader; I'm pretty good at not winding up with unwanted stuff. Recently, I learned from a good friend that sometimes you can actually trade away negative things. I have some jealousy I'd like to get rid of, but it isn't one of those things somebody else wants, so it often just sits around my heart and stinks things up. It causes me to judge and envy and resent sometimes. None of those things are attractive, productive, or "disciple-ish," but I didn't know what to do with it. That's where my friend came to the rescue. She had one simple idea from a favorite pastor, and she gladly shared (not traded) the advice with me. She said that through prayer, jealousy could be traded away to the Father who loves me with all his heart. The trade was simple: I give him all my jealousy … in exchange for gratefulness. One of the shortest and most powerful prayers we can pray is "Thank you, God!"

It was that simple! The pastor told her that the bigger our jealousy is, the smaller our gratefulness, so you trade one for the other. I've been working with my new trade, and it's true. If I'm jealous of someone else's stuff or opportunities, then I'm not being grateful for my own. If I'm busy comparing my situation, bank balance, or workload with the next person's, I'm not being grateful for all the blessings God has given me.

There are two nuggets of wisdom I've learned over the years that always help me find my balance when jealousy and complaining begin to creep into my heart. The first came from a great principal who often said, "Complaining is the greatest form of selfishness." The second nugget came from another principal, who lovingly pointed out: "Everyone is either walking through a blessing or a shadow. We're not meant to dwell forever in either." He would remind us that before we got jealous of someone's perceived blessing, we needed to stop and consider that we knew nothing about the shadow they've passed through.

The Father has a journey plotted out for each of us that leads to our sainthood, and they are all so vastly different. The joy lies in that we are perfectly made to do the Father's will, and we are given every gift, talent, and grace to live out our sainthood. It's a good idea to take St. Francis de Sales's advice: "Let us be what God wants us to be, provided we are his, and let us not be what we would like to be, contrary to his intention." Being who we were created to be means we walk with the Father through the good, bad, easy, hard, and everything in between, knowing it's all designed to lead us to heaven, not to be traded or wished away.

When I look at things through the lens of those two nuggets, I realize how absolutely and completely loved I am and that there isn't one single thing in my life I'd trade for a fancier, more expensive, newer, or flashier anything! Gratefulness is way better than jealousy. It reminds me of how much better Mom's cookies were than that stupid Twinkie. I may not have marble countertops, but I have an awesome husband who is my rock. I may not have a dream vacation to take, but I have three grown, married kids who have brought our family fabulous grandbabies, and all that makes my present days greater than any dream vacation. I may not have a closet filled with fancy clothes, but my body is wrapped with loving hugs from family and friends. I may not have treasures to be sold, but I have freedom, love, faith, and a life I get to share with people I love. Jealous? That's as crazy as a Twinkie snagged in a bad trade!

To grow in joyful prayerfulness: Start a list of things you are grateful for. Include it all — big stuff, small stuff, and everything in between. Keep the list handy and add to it every time you think of something. Use it to help you trade the negative things, the things that pull us away from the love of the Father.

St. Francis de Sales, pray for us!

34
Desire

And the world passes away, and the lust of it; but he who does the will of God abides for ever. — 1 John 2:17

Have you ever wanted something so much it occupied your thoughts completely? Sometimes we want something so badly that we pray for it, and we think about it, and we ask others to pray for it too. It's almost as if the desire overcomes our thoughts and emotions. I'm sure I'm not the only person to say that something I desired didn't materialize at all. God is so smart! He often denies those desires because he has something so much better in store for us. But when we're stuck in the middle of the wanting, that concept can be pretty tough to swallow. We desire all kinds of things: romance, money, health, jobs, a bigger house, a baby, a better car, or peace in our family. Whatever the desire, God hears and has a plan in motion. For everyone stuck in the desiring process, I came across this little story that illustrates exactly what we need to desire first.

A young man sought out the counsel of a wise and holy hermit. He asked the holy man to tell him how to find God. "How great is your desire to know him?" asked the saintly old man. "More than anything else in the world," came the young man's reply. The hermit took the young man to the lakeshore, and they waded into the water until they were neck deep. The hermit then took the young man and pushed him under the water. The young man struggled terribly, but the old man did not release his grip until the young man was about to drown. When they returned to the shore, the hermit asked the young man, "Son, when you were underwater, what did you want more than anything else?" The young man replied, "Air!" "Well, then, you will find God when your desire for him is as great as your desire for air was while I was holding you under the water."

As I'm busy praying for the things I desire, and praying for the things other people desire, I realize I'm falling short. I'm falling short because I don't quite have my desires in order. I need God; I worship, praise, and thank God all throughout my day, but my desire for him falls short. After reading that little story, I realize that if I'm being completely honest, I don't desire God as much as the young man desired air. If I worked on that desire with fervent prayer and dedication, the rest of the desires on my list would probably fall right into place because I would want only him, and in wanting him, I want less for myself. I think I would experience an enormous feeling of contentment if I got my desires in order. As I struggle to do just that, I know there will be days I completely miss the mark.

The great heroes of our faith would probably say the same thing. The evil one likes nothing more than for us to cave in to discouragement, so the wise St. Francis de Sales offered this powerful thought, and it brings encouragement to all of us battling for holiness: "Have patience with every one, but especially with yourself. I mean, do not be over-troubled about your imperfections, but always have courage enough at once to rise up again when you fall into any of them. I am very glad to hear that you begin afresh every day. There is no better means for persevering in the spiritual life than continually to be beginning again, and never to think that one has done enough." These beautiful words and this little story caused me to think a lot about what it means to desire our good God more than air. Maybe this is just what you needed today too. So, let's take a deep breath and organize our desires.

To grow in joyful prayerfulness: Read the story again and then make a list of your desires. Put the words "God > Air" at the top and spend the week praying about it all.

St. Francis de Sales, pray for us!

35
Soap and Prayer

Wash me, and I shall be whiter than snow. — Psalm 51:7

We know God will always give us exactly what we need, at precisely the time we need it — but there still may be times when we feel that he's not listening. In times of trial and suffering, we can feel as though faith and prayer are not helping. If you are struggling with something, and doubt and fear are creeping into your thoughts, consider this little story.

A soap-maker and a pastor were chatting and walking one day. The soap-maker pointed out all the pain, suffering, corruption, and dishonesty in the world. He asked the pastor how, after years of teaching about the Father's goodness and kindness and after all his sermons on God's love, mercy, and forgiveness, he could still believe that faith and prayer are relevant. The soap-maker pointed out that it clearly seemed like nonsense because in the couple thousand years since Jesus died, the world hadn't really gotten better. The pastor listened and then stopped to point out a group of little boys playing; they were covered in dirt from head to toe. The pastor told the soap-maker that clearly soap didn't work because if it did, those little boys wouldn't be so dirty. The soap-maker of course protested and pointed out that all the soap in the world wouldn't do any good unless you invested in it and used it regularly. The pastor winked and told him that the same was true of prayer and faith.

I have lots of prayer books, my shelves are stuffed with spiritual reading, I go to Mass a few times a week, and I even teach in a Catholic school … but do I always apply and appreciate my faith properly? Like the soap-maker, I wonder if it's all really working. But then I realize I need to follow the good sense of the pastor and stop and ask if I am really working. I'm inclined to think faith and prayer are working only when I'm getting what I want. After hearing this little story, I pondered how quickly I cry in despair when stuff gets messy. I pondered how quickly I think God isn't listening when I'm stuck in something hard and disappointing. I'm quick to think I'm getting a raw deal and that I'm taking more of a hit than anyone around me; I start to think, "Hmm, is this how much God loves me?"

As I was stuck in this pity-poor-me phase, I came across the words of the Prophet Nehemiah, who simply said, "It came to pass" (1:1, Douay-Rheims). There it is. The good, the bad, the hard, the easy … it all comes to pass. St. Francis de Sales said, "Yesterday may not be the judge of today, nor to-day of yesterday: all will be really judged at the Last Great Day." Our God is in the present moment, and he works in all things.

When we feel as though he's not hearing us because things are not at all stacking up the way we planned, there are a couple of things to remember. First, he always hears! His response might be "Not yet" or "Wait … I have something better," but he always hears us. The second thing to realize is that sometimes things are uncomfortable and unplanned for us because he's working through us to attend to one of his other children. His every action means something, and the meaning is far greater and the impact far more grace filled when we cooperate.

After thinking about all this and trying to decide if the

soap-maker or the pastor had the stronger case, I remembered the directions for every bar of soap: lather, rinse, repeat. All three steps are necessary to clean up those dirty little boys the men saw along their walk, and the same is true for our faith and our prayer. The more intensely we scrub with the soap, the spiffier the outcome will be. The more intensely and frequently we cry out in supplication and thanksgiving, the more we will begin to see the results of God's work. Maybe we should all put a bar of soap on our prayer table for a while!

To grow in joyful prayerfulness: Ponder this story in prayer a few times this week and ask God where you might need a little soap.

St. Francis de Sales, pray for us!

36
Quite a Challenge

Do not be conformed to this world but be transformed by the renewal of your mind, that you may prove what is the will of God, what is good and acceptable and perfect. — Romans 12:2

It started with a story that just took root in my heart about a criminal who admittedly deserved his life sentence. His heart was hard, but after decades in prison and the unrivaled power and mercy of Jesus, he changed. In his seventies, after over fifty years behind bars, he met a man who had something he had never seen and that he desperately wanted for himself. The younger man had been unjustly sent to prison for financial crimes. He was a fall guy and certainly no danger to society, but he chose to embrace the sentence as an opportunity to examine his life, his gifts, and his service to the Lord. He spent hundreds and hundreds of hours in the prison chapel adoring Jesus in the Blessed Sacrament, and this transformed him to a man of joy, gratitude, contentment, and humility. The older prisoner recognized that the young man was different and asked how to get what he had. The younger man told him he needed to spend one hour a day in adoration for thirty straight days. He was to take no Bible, Rosary, prayer book, or music. It was to be simply a time of emptying and listening. On the thirtieth day, the older prisoner experienced a dramatic, complete transformation.

The priest who shared the story then challenged everyone listening to commit to thirty minutes a day for thirty days. The ultimate goal is to give God the opportunity to speak to us about the ways he's calling us to grow in holiness. The concept of universal holiness, or holiness for all, was something St. Francis de Sales wrote about often. He believed that holiness was reserved not for the ordained or consecrated religious but for each and every one of us because it leads to greater love for the Father, and our hearts are fastened to what we love.

This whole story just sat there for nearly six weeks before I finally decided to accept the challenge. I decided to wait for the New Year, but then I got busy, and by the time I finally got myself to church to do the first day, it was already January 6. I started my time feeling bad about taking so long to get started, but then I realized that it was the feast of the Epiphany, which means "a sudden, striking revelation." Knowing God's timing is always perfect, I began to realize that the next thirty days were going to be anything but ordinary. The act of walking into church for thirty minutes without anything to pray with or guide my thoughts was pretty strange at first, but it quickly became a source of peace and freedom. I loved that there was nothing expected or required or prescribed. I just showed up to listen and be his.

Earlier that fall, I had begun to pray an odd little prayer. To be honest, it was just four thoughts that came from different places that all landed in one prayer. It actually took weeks to say those four lines and really mean them. They were a little terrifying at first, but now they are as automatic as drawing breath, and they are the lines I repeat several times as I quiet myself each time I sit before Jesus: "Wreck me. Break me. Change me. Draw me tight." For days and days, I didn't fully understand what I was inviting God to do, but one afternoon as I was playing blocks with my grandson, the Father taught through a toddler.

Once I built the block tower, my grandson took delight in wrecking it. When I rebuilt, he put cars and balls in the block pile, and I had to break away the pieces that didn't fit with the blocks. Each time I rebuilt the tower I would change the size and shape and create something new. As we were playing, a loud noise upstairs frightened Lewis, and he came running at full speed, buried his head in my neck, squeezed his little arms around me so tight, and just stayed there. It was in that moment that I understood exactly what God was leading me to in that four-line prayer. The best part was visualizing my running to my Father and the power in that clinging embrace. No matter what he was going to wreck, break, and change in my life, he'd be right there for me to cling to.

We spend so much time planning what we will do, how we'll act, what we'll change and add — but the power of the transformation of the two prisoners in the story was not "doing" but rather "letting" Jesus do the work. St. Francis de Sales had a mighty mission, and in allowing God to direct that mission, he left behind a treasury of words and practices to help to us become more prayerful and devout. Stillness and meditation are how we quiet the world enough to hear the voice of God. We don't know or need to know all the answers; we need to practice receiving what the Father has for us. Saint Francis said, "If you contemplate him frequently in meditation, your whole soul will be filled with him, you will grow in his Likeness, and your actions will be moulded on his." That is what we should be longing for.

I heard the Catholic speaker Mark Hart once say that prayer doesn't change our relationship with Jesus; "prayer is our relationship" with Jesus. I'm finding that listening, emptying, and offering for thirty minutes is very powerful prayer. Maybe you'll be like me and take a while to think it over and let it sit on your heart — but if you really want to be his, this seems a pretty great place to start.

To grow in joyful prayerfulness: Prayerfully ponder this challenge. How do you think it could transform you?

St. Francis de Sales, pray for us!

The Fifth Gift
Joyful Humility

37
St. Elizabeth of the Trinity

It seems to me that I have found my heaven on earth, because my heaven is you, my God, and you are in my soul. You in me, and I in you — may this be my motto. — St. Elizabeth of the Trinity

Humility is a quiet and powerful virtue. The distractions and comparisons that fill our days make it difficult to embrace humility and snuff out pride. Our desire to keep up and fit in can easily shift our focus from doing right to being right. Humility requires a detachment from the attitudes, judgments, and opinions of everyone but our creator. That's a tough thing to do — but it delivers peace and grace to the chaos of our days. The greatest models of humility assure us that humility is a source of freedom; through humility, we are freed from worries about the praises or condemnation of the world because we understand that we are God's.

On some level we have a desire to be noticed and included, but we have to ask ourselves by whom and for what purpose. Focusing on the Lord instead of the world helps us become humble and brings us peace and joy. Humility is about bringing glory to God, and using our gifts and talents to do that is how we thank the giver of those gifts. As humans we like to see the good fruits of our work and service, but the deep and saturating joy we're seeking comes from offering our gifts, works, prayers, and services to God and resting securely in the knowledge that his notice is all that matters.

The early part of St. Elizabeth of the Trinity's life was a continuous lesson in trading pride for humility. She had a fierce temper and a true desire to have things the way she saw fit. As she grew and learned to tame her nature, she discovered that her greatest weapons in conquering her selfish pride were quiet prayer and spiritual writing. By the time she made her first holy Communion, she was a different little girl, and the tears and joy that came to her in the Eucharist opened the doors of her heart in profound ways.

Elizabeth began dreaming and writing about joining the Carmelites, whose convent was nearby. Her desire, however, was squashed by her widowed mother. Elizabeth was severely disappointed that her mother wouldn't allow her to do what she truly felt God calling her to do. She turned to even deeper prayer to grow in humility and accept the will of the Father. The more she worked to squash her pride, the more God invited her to step away from many things. Elizabeth was an accomplished musician, and to the delight of many, she used that gift to draw others to deeper worship and prayer. When God asked her to step away from her music, she didn't hesitate, even though she longed for the peaceful connection it made her feel to the giver of the gift. From her teenage years until her early twenties, she continued to pray and to cooperate with the Father's plan, but she always prayed that it would include the opportunity to serve him as a Carmelite.

When Elizabeth turned twenty-one, her mother gave permission, and she left home and stepped into the life of a contemplative. Her writings, retreats, and prayers were powerful and humbly offered as a way to lead souls to Jesus. She was content and overjoyed that this was to be the work of her life — but in a final act of humble surrender, Saint Elizabeth died of Addison's disease just five short years after entering the Carmelite order.

True humility allows us to live in God's service, in his time, in his way, and for his glory. Saint Elizabeth, model of humility, we pray for your intercession as we try daily to trade human pride for godly humility.

St. Elizabeth of the Trinity, pray for us!

38
Be Humble

With all lowliness and meekness, with patience, forbearing one another in love. — Ephesiams 4:2

My mom was quick with one-liners. She had a way of cutting right to the chase in less than ten words, and her powerful lines had a way of knocking the wind right out of you. Those powerful lines were always spoken with great love and usually served up with a hug and a smile — and, I'm absolutely certain, a prayer — before she fell asleep that same night. Her goal was to help us get to heaven, which required heaps of humility, so she always said there was no time for messing around with the business of motherhood. One day I came home so excited that I had been given a vocal solo part for an upcoming concert. Her response still sticks in my mind like a label on a jar! She stopped peeling potatoes for a minute, smiled and told me she was proud of me, then motioned me over so she could kiss my forehead. A millisecond later she went back to peeling potatoes, saying: "Now, don't let it go to your head! Pridefulness isn't pretty on anybody!" That was her style — love hard and speak the truth, without any extra words.

As I continue to pray about what God wants me to be, he

keeps sending me back to the word *humility*. I decided to spend some time praying and reading about humility and found some stuff that is helping me realize it's much bigger than I thought. Many of the great saints have written about humility: Padre Pio, Mother Teresa, St. Francis de Sales, and Saint Benedict, to name just a few. I keep coming across a quote attributed to Saint Augustine: "It was pride that changed angels into devils; it is humility that makes men as angels." If sainthood is our mission, then humility seems to be one of tools of the trade. True humility comes when we put ourselves third. Humility is not a sign of weakness or passiveness; it's the opposite. True humility allows us to see and act like Jesus.

As I read the teachings of the great saints, I decided to squish my favorite parts together and share a few of the things I'm learning. I get the feeling that if we all acted humbly, this world would be completely transformed. Here's four ideas to start with.

First humility practice: Talk about yourself as little as possible. If we believe God truly knows the desires of our hearts, and if we do everything to please him rather than those here on earth, this makes perfect sense.

Second humility practice: Choose the more difficult or less appealing jobs. There is great humility in doing tasks nobody else wants to do. Vacuuming is one thing, but cleaning out the produce drawer with all its hidden squishy, fuzzy treasures is quite another.

Third humility practice: Don't worry about other people's business, don't talk about other people's business, and don't even be curious about things that don't concern you. We sometimes get curious and try to hear the news under the disguise of being "concerned" or "wanting to know the story so that we can pray for them," but the saints challenge us to be honest about our motives. Do we need to have our nose in someone's business, or can we use that energy to beef up our prayer life instead? Will knowing the rest of the story help us get to heaven, or will it just give us some new information we can't do something positive with?

Fourth humility practice: Recognize your talents, gifts, and graces, then promptly thank God for them and move along. We should use them well, but the ambition to be the best is not going to build our humility. I think my mom knew this one because after my first solo performance, she lovingly said: "Sweetie, that was so good, and we're proud of you, but just remember — you might sing prettier than a dozen people, but there are hundreds that sing better than you. So thank God for the gift and don't let your imagination turn you into a rock star."

Many wise people like the saints and my mom knew humility keeps us grounded, balanced, and rooted in the Lord. St. Elizabeth of the Trinity needed humility to tame her temper and strong will, and she prayed often for the gift of self-forgetful love, saying, "Yes, I believe that the secret of peace and happiness is to forget oneself … to throw oneself into the arms of God glorifies him more and gives him more joy than all the falling back upon the self, and all the self-examination that makes it live in its wretchedness." Elizabeth is the perfect companion to help us master these four practices. If we can make progress with them, we will have fewer nights when we go to bed feeling guilty or embarrassed about our pridefulness.

To grow in joyful humility: Pick one or two of these practices and sit with the Lord. Ask his help and make a plan of attack to put it into motion in your life.

St. Elizabeth of the Trinity, pray for us!

39
Little Rivets

I will make you small among the nations. — Jeremiah 49:15

Here's a little fun fact for you: Each tower of the Golden Gate Bridge contains more than 600,000 rivets. That's a lot of rivets! What on earth does that have to do with anything? This little tidbit of seemingly unimportant information grabbed my attention because it was followed by the phrase "and not one of them does something on its own."

Each rivet is absolutely important, but not a single one demands recognition for the job it does. I'd never look at a picture of the Golden Gate Bridge and say, "Oh my, look at rivet number 432,021 … isn't that an awesome rivet!" Instead, when I look at all those rivets, I realize they are an integral part of something amazing that isn't completely dependent on any one rivet. They each work together for a greater purpose. I offer this thought both as a reminder and as a comfort.

The reminder is about service, humility, and the work we do in our discipleship. I can do all kinds of personal things to grow in holiness, but if I'm not using my time, talents, and treasures to serve others, I'm not a rivet that's building the kingdom of God on earth. The Ten Commandments are divided into two groups:

love God and love others. We are called to do both. One rivet won't hold up a bridge any more than one person could single-handedly build the kingdom. This little tidbit has given me cause to consider how important a rivet I think I really am. As I type, I'm watching the sun come up through a giant airport window. It's a stunning view, and I'm so happy to be on my way to Texas to do the work the Lord's called me there to do, but I have to be careful not to think that makes my little rivet any shinier than another. After all, if a bridge was built with only one rivet, who would trust it? As I think of those 600,000 rivets, I'm reminded that strength for good work comes when the work is done by many, each doing what they are called to do in the way they're called to do it, all for the glory of God, not to be noticed as a standout.

The comfort of this little thought is that the weight of the task doesn't rest completely on one person's shoulders. We don't have to carry the weight of the world. We don't have to be in charge. We don't have to know everything, understand everything, and battle all the woes of the world on our own. Just as each individual rivet might go unnoticed, sometimes there are little places God is constantly supporting, guiding, and working in our days that may go unnoticed. Saint Elizabeth was led to a way of prayer that allowed her to share a state of stillness and deepness where she could abandon herself completely to the Father. She referred to these times as being "lost in God." In these times she could remove herself and her desires and truly see where God was working in and through her. She came to understand that the only significant thing about herself was that she was his.

God has surrounded us with lots of other rivets to share the journey and the work of our discipleship. So, relax, look around, find the rivets near you, and trust in their support. The rivets in the towers of the Golden Gate Bridge work together to support more than 112,000 vehicles a day. I'd say that's a fabulous example of combined effort. The question is: Where is God calling you to be his little rivet today?

To grow in joyful humility: Take some time in prayer to consider the kind of rivet God's calling you to be. Ponder a bit on the ideas of service, humility, and comfort from this simple idea.

St. Elizabeth of the Trinity, pray for us!

40
What's Chokin' You

Other seeds fell upon thorns, and the thorns grew up and choked them. — Matthew 13:7

When I was a little girl, I hated wearing turtleneck shirts. I felt like I was going to choke with that fabric all the way up my neck. Many a battle was waged between my mom and me on cold winter mornings due to my turtleneck phobia — and when I read this Scripture passage from Matthew, I thought of a few of those battles. I will admit that I still don't care for turtlenecks, but this verse made me stop and think about the things that choke me more than high-necked shirts.

Jesus explained to his disciples that the seed sown is the word of God planted in our hearts, and the thorns are the things in life that snuff out or diminish the work of God. It made me stop and think about the thorns in my life. What's choking my faith, making it hard to receive and grow God's word and presence? I started to make a list of all those thorns, and right away I came up with television, immoral thinking, lack of values and work ethic, and mass media. I tell you what, though — the more I thought about it, the more I realized I couldn't just blame it on "the world." Most of the thorns choking me were of my own doing. It's easy to place the blame on other people or influences, but it became obvious after a wee bit of thinking that I had plenty of thorns of my own that I needed to trim away. God made it abundantly clear that the pruning needed to start smack dab in the middle of my pride! Pride is what causes us to grip tightly to our "stuff." Sometimes God needs to prune away things that seem good and well-intentioned, but we hang on tight to them. Saint Elizabeth was a gifted musician and used her award-winning talent to bring glory to God. She used her music for Mass and leading others to deep prayer, so when the Lord asked her to give it up, she was confused but obedient to his prompting. She grieved over his request but came to realize he had other ways he was calling her to serve, and those required her to detach or be pruned.

There are many ways God is asking us to allow him to clear our gardens. Each time we gossip or tell even the tiniest lie, perhaps to make ourselves look more important or interesting, the thorns start closing in. Each time we judge others based on their appearance, status, or income, the thorns squeeze a little tighter. Each day we put our personal and social needs ahead of our prayer time, those thorns take away a little more life. Each time we fail to see others through the eyes of Christ, we stunt our spiritual growth. Complaining, criticizing, and being disrespectful are also prime fertilizer for those thorns that choke out Christ's light in our life. They are the noxious weeds that ruin the beautiful person we were created to be.

We need to tend our seeds. God put us here on earth to share his love and his light. If there is something that's choking that seed and preventing us from doing what he put us here to do, it's time to get out the tools and get to work on the thorns and weeds! It's also important to remember that humility dictates that we take care of our own thorns and weeds instead of worrying about someone else's. When my life on earth is complete, and I stand to be judged by God, I really don't think he will ask me about the thorns among my neighbor's seed. I'm quite certain I'll be accountable only for my own. When I think about the choking thorns, I need to start hacking away — turtleneck shirts almost seem comfortable in comparison!

To grow in joyful humility: Identify the things that are thorns in your life and ask God, the master gardener, to help you figure out how to uproot them so that his love can sprout and grow in your life.

St. Elizabeth of the Trinity, pray for us!

41
Three Steps

He has showed you, O man, what is good;
and what does the Lord *require of you*
but to do justice, and to love kindness,
and to walk humbly with your God? — Micah 6:8

There you have it! The Prophet Micah summed it all up in one brief verse of Scripture: Do the right thing, love things that are good, and walk humbly with God. If it's that simple, how do I manage to mess it up so often? I get all snarled up trying to make things more complicated than they need to be. I can be the queen of overthinking, and that just leads me farther away from the honest, simple root of my purpose. Anybody with me there?

Let's see if I can back up the truck and do a better job with these three simple expectations. Step one: Do the right. I guess I should ask myself, Right for whom? More often than I probably even recognize, I'm interested in doing what's right or convenient for me! I'm good at helping and praying and doing nice things when it fits in the schedule, but what about when I have to go out of my way to do good? I also need to stop and ask myself about how many times I don't do right. What if I know there is a conversation going on that I should keep my nose out of, but

I listen in anyway? What do I do if the talk turns into gossip? How do I do right and get out of that conversation? Perhaps this simple directive should keep me out of those conversations in the first place.

Step two: Love goodness. I don't think Micah was simply referring to lovely flowers and other good things found in creation. I think he was challenging us with something bigger. Here's the deal with loving goodness — it isn't always fashionable, popular, or common. Loving goodness requires us to love without judgment. It means we look for the good and Christ-like even in people who look very different than us. We can be pretty narrow in our description of what is "normal" in this society and turn a squinty eye at things that diverge from that vision. I believe the greatest sound and sight ever is a child! They are the ultimate good created by God. Not long ago I was visiting with a family who was joyfully announcing the upcoming birth of their seventh child, and I was so excited for them and honored to share in their joy. That baby will be the most loved child on the planet! As I walked away from the family, I overheard two women speaking critically about them. One woman said, "How do they think they are ever going to give that many children what they need? She doesn't even work, so they are doomed to a life of hand-me-downs and thrift store shoes." The tears stung in my eyes, and my heart hurt so badly I couldn't even speak. If I had that moment to relive, I would ask when designer clothes became more important in forming children of God than the overflowing love of a family. Loving goodness means having great compassion and respect for everything God created and doing everything in our power to defend it without casting worldly judgments.

Step three: Walk humbly with our God. The real trick with this one is to realize we can't be in charge! It really should read, "Walk humbly behind God." We might do a better job if we remember that we can't be first in our Christian walk; God himself must occupy that spot. Walking humbly means coming to terms with the fact that we are nothing without him, and the more we give him credit for, the more he blesses us. It can be tough work to step away from our pride if we don't understand the reason we're doing it. Being second is easier when we remember who is first.

St. Elizabeth encourages us to remember that we put Christ first out of love. She said: "Believe that he loves you. He wants to help you himself in the struggles which you must undergo. Believe in his love, his exceeding love." God doesn't need our approval or our praise to build him up and support his ego or self-esteem. He needs praise and adoration from us so that we can practice humility and submission to his will in our lives.

To grow in joyful humility: Pick one of the three ideas from this reading from Micah and put it to work this week. Ask the Holy Spirit to help you choose the one your soul needs most!

St. Elizabeth of the Trinity, pray for us!

42
I Want What They Have

There is great gain in godliness with contentment. — 1 Timothy 6:6

Have you ever gone out to eat with a person who has to look at every plate that comes out of the kitchen before he can decide what to order? That same person usually stares down each plate at the table, asking five questions about each order, and, more often than not, that same person can be heard saying something like, "I wish I would have ordered that instead; I want what they have!" Let's face it; if we're being totally honest, we probably make a dozen comparisons each day. We compare tiny things like parking spots and lunch choices, and we compare big things like cars, paychecks, and homes. Have you ever stopped to think about why we do this?

If we took a survey of one hundred people and asked the question "What word best describes you right now?" what percentage of people do you think might reply with the word *content*? I would be willing to bet very few, if any, would spit out that answer! We are a restless people by nature. We spend a lot of time and energy comparing, evaluating, and calculating everything. Is it greed, lust, or materialism — or is it possible that the restlessness is simply a yearning for God to fill a spot in our lives we may not even realize is vacant?

I love my life! I love everything about it, my husband, my children, my grandchildren, my work, my family, my parish, my home … my life is absolutely more blessed than I ever imagined it could be. So you would think I would be perfectly content, right? Most of the time I am, but every now and again that restless ache creeps in and makes me compare what I have with something God blessed someone else with. God has given me way more than enough, and he certainly has given me way more than I deserve, but sometimes I want him to give me that vacation to a beautiful beach resort or the spiffy new fancy thing my neighbor has. He has generously given me gifts and blessings, and I try to use them to further his kingdom. But sometimes I really wish those gifts could land me a speaker booking at a big-name conference or a holy place pilgrimage where I could rub elbows with the big names and be a part of all the exciting hoopla that goes with.

Ninety-nine days out of one hundred I'm grateful and content, but not long ago I was having that day when I was restless and feeling a little jealous. I needed to get out from under the burden of those feelings, so I slipped in the side door of the church during lunch and asked God to take them away. As I sat in the silence, the word *why* just kept popping into my head. I thought and thought about it and kept wondering things like "Why … why did he get that, and why did she get to go there, and why …" I went through the whole list, and then it hit me! The *why* meant something completely different. God was leading me to ask myself, "Why do I want those things?" He was asking, "If you really want to use the gifts I gave you to serve me, why do you care about those things?" I sat a bit longer and thought about why I wanted all those things I thought he had forgotten to give me. I told him I felt as though I was being "skipped over." As I prayed, I remembered a story I had read about Saint Elizabeth. She wanted nothing more than to be a Carmelite nun, and again and again that desire was fueled and confirmed by the Lord. But her mother would not give her permission, so she patiently waited, prayed, and served. When she was finally allowed to join the sisters, her parish priest told her he was grateful she had waited, because she had been so powerful in serving the troubled youth who truly needed her gifts.

Then the train hit me. I was wandering away from God's truth. Unlike Saint Elizabeth, I wanted to use my gifts the way I wanted to. But he doesn't allow me to write so that I can be recognized; he gave me this gift to spread his love and help others recognize his presence. He didn't give me my speaking gift to become recognized in a faraway fancy place; he gave it to me to speak to whomever he puts in the chairs wherever he sends me. He didn't send me to a beach; he sent me to spread his love to a school building full of children. He didn't forget to give me a fancy car or the income for a beautiful cottage; he gave me exactly what I needed to provide me with the perfect balance of humility and peace. Mostly, he made me realize that he has blessed me with the perfect life for me! What I need and what everyone else needs are as different as can be, but in the difference lies the perfection that only he can determine.

I left the church that afternoon knowing that the *why* really meant: Why are you restless for things that aren't yours? He uncovered the restlessness in my soul that needed to rest in him! I think I'll swap *C* words — I'll swap "compare" for "content." Each time I'm tempted to say, "I want what they have," I'll say instead, "God, thank you for taking such perfect care of them because You know perfectly what we need!" He works in ways both huge and tiny based on things we will never see or know. Thank you, Father, for being in charge — you always get it right!

To practice joyful humility: Practice gratitude this week and pray for the grace to be content. Ask God each time you are tempted to make a comparison to settle your restless soul!

St. Elizabeth of the Trinity, pray for us!

43
Third Place

But seek first his kingdom and his righteousness, and all these things shall be yours as well. — Matthew 6:33

When was the last time you heard someone scream in an excited voice, "Yeah, I'm third! Woohoo for me!" Probably never — that's just nuts. Or is it? We live in a world that promotes being first, best, biggest, and fastest. Being third is nothing to aspire to by most standards, or so I thought. I was reading an article recently, and in small print at the bottom of one of the pages was a quote from the author, who said she constantly strives to be third: God first, others second, and herself third.

I chewed on that thought for the better part of two days. My first reaction was, "Oh yeah, good idea. I do that too." Then reality whapped me upside the head, and I was flooded with examples of times I truly was not content with third place. God is so good at putting me in my place. Then I moved on to this thought: Well, surely it doesn't mean third all the time? For instance, it's my obligation to be the best mother and wife I can be, so I have to try to be the best or first in that role. Then I thought about my teaching. Surely God and a whole batch of parents each year want me to be the best teacher for their children? Imagine the gasps at open house if I proudly announced I was the third-best teacher. I then proceeded to go into the pattern I usually go into when I hear something from God I don't really want to agree with. I decided the quote was flawed or goofy.

Usually at that point, I have to give up and ask God why he really led me to the words and begin to open my mind and heart to the truth he's speaking through them. He didn't fail me! After some pouting, praying, and processing, I got the truth. The truth is that it isn't about me at all! God has to come first, or my life is nothing but one long chain of goofed-up stuff. God always has to be in the front seat because I'm a lousy navigator and take way too many wrong turns and dead-end paths. He never loses the way. If I believe he will lead me perfectly in anything I do in his name, then it's easier to let him claim first place.

If I can agree to that, then I have to remember that the greatest commandment is to love others. Saint Elizabeth was so committed to the Trinity that she knew the greatest way to love God and love others was to help lead them to a deeper encounter with Christ. This is the most basic thing he asks of us, and honoring his request to love him by loving others means putting others in spot two. Isn't this the least I can do for the God who has done everything for me? That leaves third place — and instead of selfishly looking at it as a consolation prize, I had to stop a minute and realize those first two places were for him and in service to him, so third place is as close to him as I could possibly be. After thinking it over, I really like third place. If I'm doing everything I do to serve him and the people he created, then how can I want anything more? If I let him be first and offer everything I do to him, it will all be just as he wishes, and that will always be right.

Thinking of third place in that new way is very freeing. The pressure is off. I just have to follow along behind first and second with a heart full of love, and I will win every time. I'll just stay locked in third and glide along on his tailwind. The journey to heaven is a great one … and the prize for coming in third is magnificent. Bronze just became my new favorite color!

To grow in joyful humility: Spend some serious time this week pondering which spot you're in. How can you work harder to come in third?

St. Elizabeth of the Trinity, pray for us!

44
You're Not Her

After me comes a man who ranks before me. — John 1:30

Have you ever heard the phrase "Be careful what you wish for"? A humble heart is something I pray for constantly, and I laugh at the frequency of God's lessons. Recently, I was in the lobby of a convention center after I had given a talk, and a lady came up to me. She gave me a hug and said, "Your message really touched my heart; will you take a selfie with me?" I stood right beside her, and she held up her phone to snap our picture. As soon as she had it in place, she said, "Oh, wait, you're not her — I thought you were someone else." We laughed and went in different directions.

Selfies make up a pretty large and humorous number of overall posts on my Facebook and Instagram feeds. These quickly snapped images capture important moments, achievements, or places, and they give the viewer a tiny little snapshot of someone else's life. I'll make a confession — I have never posted a selfie, because I need more time to pose and make sure I don't look as though I have three chins or a neck the size of a tree trunk. By the time I get just the right photo angles lined up, the moment's long over! Selfie overload can cause us to think our life isn't quite as exciting as the folks posting dozens of selfies in fancy, fun places. If we get too tangled up in the likes and shares and comments from our selfie posts, keeping our humility in check can get a little tough.

Humility can be a tricky thing to master. Our culture screams, "Be the best!" We seem to focus constantly on who's influencing others and leading the pack, but the first chapter of John's Gospel teaches a beautiful lesson about the exact opposite. In this competitive world, it's a bit shocking to read the words "After me comes a man who ranks before me." It's one thing to think someone is more important than you, but to announce it loud and proud to all who will hear — that just seems crazy by today's standards! The funny thing is that John the Baptist was completely comfortable with the way the events unfolded. A supporting role was perfect for him. He recognized that he had a completely different purpose than Jesus did in fulfilling God's plan. He didn't get caught up in the fact that he would be doing the baptizing and that he had been chosen to bring God's grace to the crowds. He simply saw himself as a part of something amazing. He didn't feel the need to be the star or have folks notice his good works.

John wasn't the main attraction; he was meant to prepare the way and take part in the mighty work of the Father and his Son. Like St. John the Baptist, St. Elizabeth of the Trinity understood that her job was to magnify the love of the Lord with her life. She was content just to love him and expressed her contentment by saying: "It seems to me that I have found my heaven on earth, because my heaven is in you, my God, and you are in my soul. You in me, and I in you." I'm sure if selfies had been taken the day that John announced the Lamb of God, John would have been nowhere to be found. He wanted no notice, no thanks, no acknowledgment. John opened the door, so to speak, so that the Father, Son, and Holy Spirit could enter and add an amazing chapter to the love story God shares with us. Today is a great day to ask yourself, What are my motives for serving the Lord? Do I do it for him, or do I do it so that others might notice I'm a part of things? Am I trying to be his servant, or am I trying to be a star?

To grow in joyful humility: Take this little prayer with you into your quiet moments with the Lord this week:

> Loving Father, please help me push past my pride. Give me the grace to love and serve you with a humble heart. Please allow me to see those who need your mercy and your love, and show me how to help them make room for you so that you can be the star in their life. Amen.

St. Elizabeth of the Trinity, pray for us!

45
Empty Cups

But he said to me, "My grace is sufficient for you, for my power is made perfect in weakness." I will all the more gladly boast of my weaknesses, that the power of Christ may rest upon me. — 2 Corinthians 12:9

I have seen these words several times lately: "You can't pour from an empty cup." There is truth to that saying, and I think the original intent was great. It's important to take care of yourself. But the more I think about it, the more it bugs me — I found that when looking from the perspective of a humble disciple, it seems completely false. I scratched my head, wondering why I was reacting so stubbornly to a line meant for good. After lots of thought and prayer, I realized God was using this line to get under my skin and remind me of some important things I had been forgetting. Very often the Gospel and the worldview are pretty different!

The truth is that yes, you can! We do it all the time. As parents, teachers, and friends, we often give even when we don't think there is anything left in the tank. If a child comes to me frustrated and hurting, I'm sure not going to look at her and say, "Sorry, child, please come back when I've had a little 'me' time." If a coworker, parent, or friend stops in to share his struggles, I'm not going to ask him to come back after I've taken a nap. Teaching during a pandemic stretched me so far that I thought I'd snap, but as teachers we always keep finding a little more in the cup to pour out. As parents, we are called to do the same again and again and again. We just keep pouring, hoping there are enough drops left to get us through the day. Jesus, Mary, the saints … they showed us what it looks like to humbly love and follow the Father, trusting that he will, in his amazing providence, give us what our faithful hearts need.

The world would have us believe that success depends on our effort and energy. The world would have us believe that we deserve to be happy, that we have to carve out that happy time ourselves, and that we deserve to take time for ourselves to recharge so that we can do more stuff. The world would have us believe that if our cups aren't full, we will crumble up in a heap in the corner somewhere. The world would have us believe it is all up to us, and if we don't take care of ourselves, nobody else will. As usual, the world doesn't get it right! Thank goodness we have something more truthful, hopeful, and joyful to turn to: a Father who loves us so enormously we will never be empty. He has created us for love, and he will make certain we have all we need to do the work we were created to do. We need to depend on this truth and keep on loving even when we're tired or discouraged. Trusting him means we never fear emptiness but delight in the opportunities we are given to love others in our words and actions. Saint Elizabeth often included these words in her prayers: "May my life be a continual prayer, a long act of love."

The Father lovingly reminded me that he's in charge of my cup. It is precisely in those moments when I feel I have nothing left to give that I'm supposed to turn to him. He will give me everything I need, everything he's asking me to give to one of his children. He will give me more than enough. His love, his grace, and his compassion are more than enough! Way too many days we feel as though we're giving all we have, and he lets us, because our stubborn pride blinds us, and it isn't until we hit empty that we can get out of his way. We only cry out and let God do things the right way after we have tried forty-three dozen wrong ways.

If we approached Jesus in humility at the first sign of distress, instead of waiting until we feel empty and frazzled, things would work much better. Pray continuously throughout the day as you pour again and again from your cup — sometimes, we pour out in places he hasn't called us to pour.

Jesus said, "The Son of man also came not to be served but to serve" (Mk 10:45). Those words are our mission on earth too. I'm supposed to serve God and serve others, and the emptier my cup, the more I have done the work the Father put me on this earth to do. That should bring me a joy that fills my cup to overflowing. This life really isn't about me at all, and I needed to be reminded of that. Worrying about my cup and expecting to always "feel good" about life is crazy. Trusting that the Father will always make sure I have what I need to pour brings a sense of peace and contentment to these crazy days. I think the saying should be "I serve a God who always fills my cup!"

To grow in joyful humility: Spend a few extra minutes in prayer these next days, and don't forget to take your cup to the Father for a refill.

St. Elizabeth of the Trinity, pray for us!

The Sixth Gift
Joyful Peace

46
St. Gianna Beretta Molla

The secret of happiness is to live moment by moment and to thank God for all that He, in His goodness, sends to us day after day. — St. Gianna Beretta Molla

Our lives are in an ever-shifting season of blessings and shadows, and our peace depends on knowing that God is with us in both. It's not as if one is a punishment and the other a reward. Both are the recipe for growing in holiness. Saint Gianna is a glowing hero when it comes to showing us how to live the seasons of life with peace and grace and faith. She suffered, rejoiced, served, and loved peacefully all at the same time in every season because she knew God was bigger and would lovingly use everything for good. Peace doesn't mean everything is in the calm order we expect ... perfect peace comes from seeking and trusting the Father in the midst of all the storms and situations. Peace springs from trust and patience, all working together to bring us joy.

Saint Gianna demonstrated a peaceful, beautiful ability to wait for the Lord. She lived her life steeped in faith and peacefully seeking the will of the Father. She did many things that society might consider impressive. She was a successful doctor, wife, and mother during an age when doing all those things was not common or met with great support. What I find most inspiring about her, however, is that these things didn't all come in the normal form and fashion — nor did her joyful, peaceful demeanor reflect all she endured and overcame that, to much of the world, probably went unnoticed.

Saint Gianna was a doctor, but she had to give up a summer of hiking and adventure — things that brought her heart peace and contentment — to complete remedial summer school classes; hardly a path you'd expect for a doctor. She enjoyed a glorious wedding day as a lovely bride, but she was older than the typical age of a bride in her day. She had an inspiring God-centered marriage, but it was peppered with the difficulty of her husband's hectic work travel and the demands of her own medical practice. She was an adoring mother, but prior to the arrival of each of her beloved babies, she suffered nine months of wretched sickness and physical strain while still lovingly caring for her family and patients. Her fourth and final pregnancy required the sacrifice of her very life, a sacrifice she made with the grace and peace of the Father rooted securely in her heart.

Saint Gianna followed God's plan with a stillness in her soul. She met every twist and turn of her life with prayer and calmly waited for his guidance. While she waited, she asked how he wanted her to wait, to move forward, and to serve. She paused and prayed rather than forging and forcing her way through her days. She served and loved through her fatigue, disappointment, sickness, and fear. While she nurtured and tended her marriage, children, patients, and her powerful vocation, she was peacefully working her way toward sainthood one prayerful yes at a time.

Saint Gianna, we prayerfully ask your intercession to help us be still and peacefully wait for the ways God is planning to work in us and through us.

St. Gianna Beretta Molla, pray for us!

47
Thanks for the Peace, Saint Paul

Finally, brethren, rejoice. Mend your ways, heed my appeal, agree with one another, live in peace, and the God of love and peace will be with you. — 2 Corinthians 13:11

If we're looking for the true answer to all that troubles us today, it seems to be right here in this Scripture passage: Rejoice, encourage each other, agree with each other, live in peace. That's the opposite of what's happening these days, and it's all giving me a giant headache. Every time I turn around, it seems there is another line in the sand and a group of folks screaming at us to pick a side. Why? Is there a prize for being on the "right side" of an argument that makes no sense to begin with? Some issues absolutely do have clear right and wrong sides, but that's not what I'm talking about. I'm talking about the stuff that stirs up fear and anxiety, the stuff that is based on half-truths and opinion, the stuff that is dividing us for no good reason and sucking away our peace.

I saw a headline the other day that said, "Where is God now?" I was surprised to find the perfect answer to that question in this reading from Paul to the Corinthians. Where is God? Well, he's with you, and he's measured out his love and his peace in huge heaps if we do one simple thing — live in peace. Peace is a choice we have to make, sometimes several times a day. When we check social media and get wound up over something, we have to stop and say, "Jesus, bring me your peace." Instead of firing back a reply or comment to someone's argument, stop and say, "Jesus, bring me your peace." When you read an article or hear a story about violence, unrest, and blame, stop and say, "Jesus, bring me your peace, and, Jesus, bring your peace to _____." If we're arguing and dividing and proving and blaming, we won't find peace; in fact, we'll create a heaping scoop of the opposite.

Paul gave the Corinthians these words of wisdom and encouragement a couple thousand years ago, and, golly, do we still need them today! Encourage others, seek peace, and the love and peace of Christ will fill you. There is so much nonsense going on right now — if we stopped and thought about these short words and prayed for peace each time we got ruffled, that would be a big hunk of time spent doing something that will actually make us feel better. And there are thousands of us looking for a way to feel better! Saint Gianna lived a life that pointed to the peace of Christ, and her wise words offer simple direction for all of us today seeking peace. She said: "The stillness of prayer is the most essential condition for fruitful action. Before all else, the disciple kneels down." When we feel our peace slipping away, entering into quiet prayer can be powerful for sure.

God is not absent right now. He's not on a luxury cruise or hiking in a remote mountain range. He's truly present and busy in the middle of all the mess, but we must seek him out. We need to go where he is, in the peace, the encouragement, the positive, the light. That's tough to do some days. But the effort is worth it, and our souls will thank us when we seek his peace instead of getting stuck in the mess. This is our cross to bear. Slugging our way through the ugly and the uncertain in our world right now is our way to grow in holiness. Growing in holiness takes effort. Words like these from Saint Paul help break things down into simple, doable parts if we grab them. If you'd like a little inspiration from a wise disciple living a little closer to our time, here is some wisdom from an "almost nun" who lived through World War II and stepped into motherhood with nearly a dozen children who were not her own. Maria von Trapp said, "We shall be together with the man of Nazareth, who will recognize us as his disciples if we now patiently bear our daily cross."

Where is God in all this? He's right there, waiting to help us pick up our daily cross so that he can lead us toward peace. As we walk together through our day with those crosses, let's take Saint Paul's advice and sprinkle some more encouragement and a little less arguing into our days.

To grow in joyful peace: Call or text someone today with a word of encouragement. For extra "peace points," make it someone you don't always agree with.

St. Gianna Beretta Molla, pray for us!

48
It's Time to Behold

Be still, and know that I am God. — Psalm 46:10

Have you ever noticed how life comes in seasons? I'm talking not just about weather and months but about the seasons of family, relationships, and our heart. Some seasons are slower and happy and give us moments to laugh and reflect, while others are filled with high-gear, white-knuckle action. Whether the season is easy or tough, God is right there, teaching and guiding us through it. I will be the first to admit that sometimes I don't see him, and my shifts from season to season are not very attractive or graceful, so I found myself praying for greater peace and balance in my shifting.

Recently I was in the middle of a tricky season shift, and I found myself at Mass listening to a homily that was God being fancy exactly when I needed it most. The priest mentioned that the word *behold* is spoken before something new and amazing is about to happen in the Mass and in Scripture. It hit my heart, so I prayed that the Father would help me find peace in the changing of all the seasons of life and look at the beginning of each new season as a "behold day." To embrace the "behold days" of our life, we should be prepared for the fact that some will usher in lovely things, and others will be harder to head into. Saint Gianna said, "Love and sacrifice are closely linked, like the sun and the light. We cannot love without suffering, and we cannot suffer without love." In celebrating the behold day of a season I wasn't fond of, I learned a few things:

- Time doesn't slow down; you have to do the slowing. There will always be stuff going on, but stillness is where God can find you and bring peace.
- Things can get done without me. I've never been very good at saying no, but my no makes way for someone else to say yes.
- Life comes in stages or seasons just as books come in chapters. You'll never get to the great ending if you don't keep turning the pages and following along.
- My screen porch is not just architecture and a lawn chair storage area. It's for sitting, praying, rocking grandkids, visiting with friends and neighbor kids, writing, and reading, even in the middle of the day when there are chores to be done.
- The more you make time for quiet stillness, the greater the peace. The greater the peace, the greater the contentment, and with contentment comes clearer perspective, less stress, a more prayerful heart, and a happier demeanor. Who knew!

I feel a little as if I'm in a lawn chair parked in shallow ocean water. Life is rolling by, and the waters are changing and washing over me. Sometimes it feels like warm waves and a gentle breeze, and other times the waves are high and heavy, but it's always God whose hand is stirring the waves. My prayer on each new "behold day" is "God, help me be still. I'm lousy at it!" Busy isn't always a choice, but stillness is. Perhaps it's the best choice we can make as we settle into the next season so that we can find him and his plan as we behold the peace and newness of the season.

To grow in joyful peace: Look at the week ahead and choose three chunks of time where you will commit to being still and quiet. Pray that the Lord meets you powerfully in those moments.

St. Gianna Beretta Molla, pray for us!

49
Just Rockin'

Come to me, all who labor and are heavy laden,
and I will give you rest. — Matthew 11:28

I love rocking chairs. My favorite place to rock is outside on a porch or a patio. When I have the chance to sit and rock, peace and calm just seem to wash over me. It's funny how quickly you fall into a gentle rhythm when you rock — something often missing from the chaos of our days. There are a lot of things we do quickly, but rocking in a rocking chair isn't really one of them. It's funny how just a few minutes of gently moving back and forth can cause you to slow your roll and breathe.

In all honesty, I've never really thought too much about rocking until this weekend. I was sitting in a rocking chair on a patio looking out at the dry Texas prairie, just taking in all the beauty of the reddish-brown dirt and dry landscape. I noticed as I rocked that it was so flat that I could see for miles. I sat there soaking it all in, watching a couple of rabbits hopping around among the rose bushes. It was dry and hot, but the wind was blowing a bit, so I didn't really notice the heat. The view was beautiful in its own way. As I rocked, it occurred to me that just the weekend before I had been rocking in West Virginia, and the view was so very different. As I rocked there, I looked out on tree-covered mountains. Everything was green, and there were flowers of every color within my view. From that rocker I could also see and hear two beautiful fountains. I remember just sitting there soaking it all in until the mosquitoes chased me inside.

As I rocked away in West Texas, thinking about rocking in West Virginia, I thought about rocking on my own front porch looking out at the cornfield as we chatted with the neighbors who stopped by for a visit. Truth be told, I've rocked in a lot of different places. I got the chance to rock on the porch with my dad and my brother, who live more than six hundred miles away. I've rocked and prayed. I've rocked and laughed. I've rocked and sipped hot coffee. And the night before I'd rocked and cried as I prayed for the soul of my good friend's dad who lost his battle with cancer. I've rocked babies to sleep and listened to the tales of people I love.

The Father has used something I love to teach me something important. Saint Gianna as a mother was no stranger to rocking and no doubt spent many hours rocking to soothe fussy little ones, while seeking comfort for herself as well, as she navigated her way through very difficult pregnancies. Her rocking, I'm sure, flowed into the gentle rhythm of her deep prayer and affection for the Father. I often imagine the strength it took for her to rock her babies during her fourth pregnancy, contemplating the uncertainty and danger ahead, and I'm sure she rocked to ease the hurt in her heart after two miscarriages. I bet she grew in trust and peace with each creak of the chair.

As I pondered all my rocking, it occurred to me that those times stick so vividly in my mind because they all have something in common: I slowed down and opened my eyes to what was around me. In the slow, gentle rhythm of the rocker, I was able to soak in the beauty of my surroundings. I was able to soak in the presence of those rocking with me. I was able to just be still, shut up, and take it all in. When I think about it, I was really seeing God and his goodness in the Texas prairie and the West Virginia mountains and the Clinton County corn and the heavy eyes of sleepy babies. I felt the love of God as I laughed and prayed with family and friends. In a rocker I am reminded of the slow and gentle ways God is a part of the rhythm of every moment of every day. The trick, however, is to slow down and recognize it.

I love how fancy God gets sometimes with his lessons. It would have been so easy for him to make something in my life come to a crazy screeching halt to teach me to slow down, but instead he let me learn while enjoying some beautiful stuff and people all while rocking in my chair. Is he great or what!

To grow in joyful peace: Take a few minutes this week to sit in a rocking chair. Let yourself slow down and allow God to grant you some peace.

St. Gianna Beretta Molla, pray for us!

50
The Peace of an Ordinary Day

I love those who love me,
and those who seek me diligently find me. — *Proverbs 8:17*

The day was so beautiful that it caught me by surprise. I was driving to Indianapolis to pick up my daughter, and about thirty minutes into the drive I had this overwhelming feeling of peace and gratitude. The weather was perfect — blue sky, no humidity, bright sun, seventy-five degrees. In the quiet of my drive, I realized that I had no impending deadlines, no yucky task that was pressing on my time, and nowhere else I'd rather be at the moment. I couldn't help but smile, one of those really deep smiles that comes from somewhere down around your kneecaps! I just started to pray in gratitude for all the things that made it a perfect day.

As I was soaking it all in, my mind wandered to all those I love who are suffering — families with sick loved ones, families facing tough decisions, folks knee-deep in grief and struggle. I prayed for them one by one as they popped into my mind and wished they could be with me, enjoying the perfect, peaceful day

I was right in the middle of. The emotion of their pain and struggle washed over me, and I felt it in my heart, but after praying for each one, my mind and my heart went back to the peaceful, perfect day God had laid out for me.

After another hundred miles, I said out loud in my car, "Man, I wish every day could be like this!" I smiled and drove on for a while, and then it hit me. If every day was like this one, I wouldn't be struck by the peace, and I wouldn't notice the perfection of such an ordinary day. Nothing was spectacular about it. I hadn't won anything, I didn't have more money than I had the day before, and the world was still full of pockets of ugly, but the day was a gift. As I kept driving I realized that the purpose of days like this is to fill my soul with the grace, love, presence, and tenderness of my Father in preparation for days that weren't peaceful. I realized how much I had to be grateful for in both the peaceful days and the tough ones because, as Saint Gianna and her husband shared in letters to one another, "Everything is a gift from God and should be respected as a gift."

I soaked up that perfect day, and in my mind I bottled it up to put away like a treasure in my heart. The next time the day isn't so lovely or easy or perfect, I'll remember that day and know that more will come. I'll remember what it felt like and what a gift it was. It can't last forever, but then again, neither can the yucky days. I'm grateful for that day, and I wonder how many others there have been along the way that I missed. Mostly I just thank him for the glory of a peaceful, perfect, ordinary day!

To grow in joyful peace: Think about a peaceful, perfect, ordinary day you experienced and ask God to help you put that memory like a treasure in your heart to save for a day you need it.

St. Gianna Beretta Molla, pray for us!

51
Worth the Wait

And I will raise him up at the last day. — John 6:40

We live in an on-demand world. Movies, drive-through meals, pharmacies, groceries, and dry cleaning, just to name a few — we can order practically anything under the sun and have it on our front porch in two days. Waiting and being last aren't usually part of our daily routine. I'm constantly searching for ways to get things done faster and more efficiently to save time so that I can cram more stuff into my day. The rush and pace of our days can really put a wrinkle in our peace!

As I worked my way through the Gospel of the day, John 6:35–40, I got excited reading about what will come to me, what Jesus will do for me, where my faithfulness will lead me. It's such a hope-filled collection of verses. I need to see Jesus, believe in Jesus, and know that my faithfulness is what he's asking of me. Saint John lays out some beautiful steps to eternal life in this short Gospel, but then comes that ending, "the last day." I have to wait until then? What??? My fast-paced mind wondered if I could speed things up a little, because I don't like waiting, and who knows when the last day really is, anyway! As I prayed with this reading a while, I had a frightening thought followed by a beautiful memory — God knew I'd need both.

The frightening thought began to unfold as I realized how many times things came my way when I wasn't as ready or prepared as I thought I was. This usually leads to some frantic scrambling, which is not at all helpful to our peacefulness. I had a startling thought as I considered how truly unprepared I am for the last day! The Father helped me ponder all those places and things that need lots of prayer and work in my life. The weight of those thoughts was setting hard on my heart, and feelings of gigantic unworthiness and self-disappointment were about to draw me into hopelessness, but then out of nowhere I thought of a day with my grandma Thelma. Peace filled my heart as the Father allowed me to relive a lesson from my childhood, a day decades ago that filled my heart with the love of both a Father and a grandma.

When I was a little girl in Grandma's Kansas kitchen, she taught me how to make the perfect angel food cake from scratch. I remember beating all thirteen of those egg whites and how badly I wanted to crank up the hand mixer and make it go faster, but Grandma smiled and reminded me that beating all those egg whites took time, and rushing would lead to a flop. Later I lay on the floor staring through the oven window, watching that cake get taller and taller, wondering when it would be done, and she reminded me that baking it took time, and rushing would lead to a flop. Then there was the agonizingly long wait for the cooling on a glass coke bottle tipped upside-down on the counter. It seemed that it took all day, but she would pat my impatient hands and say, "Great things happen in the waiting!" She was so right! If she had indulged my impatience at any step of the process, it would have been a flop. Even though I reluctantly and perhaps a bit rebelliously followed the lead of the master cake baker, the end of that fabulous memory came sitting at the table with Grandma Thelma in the middle of the afternoon with one piece of cake and two forks. The wait led to something splendid. God is reminding me of that every day.

Waiting peacefully is a skill we need to practice daily. Grandma showed me how, and the ending was so good. But sometimes, despite all our waiting, things don't turn out the way we expected. Sometimes we wait well, and it still seems like a big flop — but God is in the flop! Saint Gianna wanted motherhood and a holy marriage; in fact, she waited past the normal age to enjoy both. Her husband and her children and her thriving pediatric practice seemed exactly what she'd waited and prayed for, but she lived only long enough to see her fourth child experience her first week of life. She sacrificed her life for that child, and some might look at her life as tragic. That daughter she sacrificed her life for is also named Gianna — she is a doctor who travels the world to share the message of her mother's commitment to the sanctity of life, the beauty of God's plan, and the peace of a humble soul. Saint Gianna died at the age of thirty-nine repeating the words, "Jesus, I love you." Her life has brought and will continue to bring countless souls to Christ. It doesn't seem so tragic when you know she's enjoying the rewards of eternal life that the rest of us are working so hard and waiting for.

So, I will keep peacefully believing, hoping, praying, and wanting him ferociously while I wait for that last day! To each day I need to add: "Loving Father, please use your gentle hand to slow me down. Grant me a spirit of peace and patience as I notice the ways you are working in my life, and help me prepare to be raised up on the last day!"

To grow in joyful peace: What are you hurrying with? Make note of the areas in your life God might be calling you to slow down and wait for him to work.

St. Gianna Beretta Molla, pray for us!

52
Puppies in a Basket

As the Father has loved me, so have I loved you; abide in my love. — John 15:9

When I think back on my decades as a teacher, I often find myself remembering classes and students who came in and out of my life. Some memories make me laugh, some make me sigh, and some make my eyes leak a little. It would be easy to get lost in these thoughts for hours, but there really isn't time to sit still and ponder for too long, or I'll be late for something! Memory lane is a lovely place to visit, but sometimes it can be a very long trip.

One day I was thinking about my vocation as a teacher, and I put those thoughts aside to read the Gospel of the day, which happened to be in John 5. As I began reading this Gospel, I remembered one class in particular that was good at lots of things, but remaining in one place for more than a split second was not their gift. Getting them to sit still and listen peacefully for any length of time was like trying to put puppies in a basket. I was convinced they were spring-loaded. Several times a day I would witness the tiny window of time they would all be still, and then one would get up, and pretty soon another would follow, and then another would wiggle off the carpet or away from the table, and before I knew it nearly all of them had escaped. I laughed and remembered those little lovelies fondly for a few minutes and wondered how many times God looks down at us and makes the same comparison.

In this Gospel, Jesus clearly teaches that the Father asks us simply to remain in his love. We don't have to run around searching for it or trying to do heroic things to earn it. The promise is simple: Remain with me, and I will bring you joyful peace. The funny thing about this message is that it sums up all we want and all we have to do to get it in a few short verses. We complicate things so terribly! Stay with me — don't run around like crazy; just be still in my presence. He made it simple enough. But getting our attention and convincing us to rest in his peace and trust in his love must be a lot like trying to put puppies in a basket. One of the nuggets of wisdom from Saint Gianna that I treasure is this: "The secret of happiness is to live moment by moment and to thank God for all he, in his goodness, sends to us each day." Life is about the moments, and those moments are precious if we're still enough to notice them.

I spent several days with this verse in prayer wanting God to help me be still and feel his peace, but the to-do list was getting longer, and my stress was getting higher. I got all the way to Friday feeling no different, and that's when I got a reminder of how much he wants me to remain in his love instead of in the chaos. I was praying at the all-school Mass that morning and feeling a little overwhelmed about all that needed to be done, so I just asked him to take over and give me the peace and strength to get things done with joy in my heart. When I got back to the classroom and checked my email, there was a message from a wonderful mom volunteering to do one of the big jobs on my to-do list. I hadn't asked for help; she just sent a message and said, "Hey, can I help with this?" The puppy in me just sat still as I said, "Thank you,

Jesus!" Wouldn't it be great at the beginning of a busy week if we decided we were going to carry the image of puppies in a basket with us? When the to-do list starts to feel overwhelming, and I'm flying from task to task like a witch on a broom, I will remember to be the one puppy who falls asleep in the basket and just peacefully rests in the Father's love and trusts in his providence.

To grow in joyful peace: Purposefully set aside ten minutes each day to sit still and think about God and all he's doing in your life. Be that puppy that climbs into the basket to be still and remain in the Father's peaceful love.

St. Gianna Beretta Molla, pray for us!

53
It's All About Balance

A false balance is an abomination to the LORD,
but a just weight is his delight. — Proverbs 11:1

I had a wonderful kindergarten teacher named Mrs. Justice, and she was a gem! Seriously, if I can remember gobs of things about her after more than a half century, she must have been awesome! I loved her laugh, her kindness, and the way her room felt so much like home. There was, however, one thing in our classroom that I hated: the balance beam. The silly thing sat just a few inches off the floor, but it terrified me. I would step up on it and instantly begin to sway and stagger as if I'd been drinking for a week. Looking back, I have no idea why I had such a lousy sense of balance. I'm sure I just thought too much about it, and the lack of balance was all in my head, but I still remember that confusing, out-of-control sensation.

I haven't been on a balance beam since kindergarten, but I sure can relate to that same out-of-balance feeling for different reasons. The funny thing is that when I was trying to walk on that silly beam, it was all my issue; I was the one responsible for that fuzzy, tippy feeling, so all I had to do was hop down, and balance was restored. Today it's not so simple. Today the imbalance and peace disruption are usually served up at the hands of others, and it can make us a little crazy.

Fake news wrecks our peace and leads us to imbalance. People with narrow-minded, black-and-white, "hell or high water" thinking and speech can lead us to imbalance. Companies or folks who only tell the slice of truth that helps them market their stuff lead us to imbalance. Last week my school computer screamed at me and flashed warnings that it had been attacked by some kind of Trojan horse, worm, scorpion, flaming-dragon virus thingy. It scared the snot out of me! I didn't really want to work on curriculum in the first place, but to then have my computer tell me that my credit cards and possibly my firstborn offspring were in danger (OK, maybe that's a little dramatic!) made me feel a little out of balance and put gigantic wrinkles in my peace. It ended up being a pretty simple fix, but the voice coming from my computer wanted to sell me some kind of product to perfect my potentially attacked computer. Wasn't that helpful of it! Once I found out everything was OK, I breathed a sigh of relief, and then I got a little irritated that it was so easy to be thrown off balance; I was right back in kindergarten facing down that silly balance beam.

After the whole virus debacle, I happened to find an article on a health and nutrition blog that outlined some of the fabulous things good black coffee can do for a person. I of course agreed enthusiastically with every word and felt very affirmed in my coffee habit. Not two hours later, I was checking email and stumbled onto an article telling me my morning "nectar of the gods" was going to have me lame, forgetful, and sick as a dog if I didn't dump it out and never take a sip again. Of course, I took that entire article as a big pile of horse pucky! Again, though, I was surprised how easy it is to lose our balance when everyone with access to social media can flip the truth completely out of wack and leave us scratching our heads.

Since I'm not queen of the universe and can't control all the ridiculous stuff people like to spit out as truth, I had to give it some prayer and thought, and this is what I came up with: Logic and common sense may seem to be out of fashion, but we can all make an effort to bring them back. Thinking first, speaking later (or not at all) would be a peaceful and prudent idea. Don't believe that everything you hear (or read) is sound advice. Trading media time for prayer time would be splendid for many reasons. The final thing — and it's a big one — is to pray for peaceful balance and truth.

We get so sucked into the craziness, but what if we just … didn't? What if we refrained from replying to something just so that we can have our voice heard? It just might be better for the whole planet if we worried more about simply having our voice heard by the Father who gave us that voice, because I'm pretty sure he didn't instruct us in Scripture to "go forth and make an ugly, controversial, half-baked truthful noise." Christ is our center of balance. No matter what the world is yelling that might throw us off our game, remember these words from Saint Gianna: "We must be living witnesses of the beauty and grandeur of Christianity." If more of us were living that way, we would make a difference. When all else fails, do what I did in kindergarten when that silly beam threw me off balance … just hop off and go do something better!

To grow in joyful peace: The next time you read something that throws off your peace and balance, stop right then and there and pray for the person or folks at the root of it. Something mighty will happen if we all get a little better at that!

St. Gianna Beretta Molla, pray for us!

54
Eyes Wide Open

Finally, brethren, whatever is true, whatever is honorable, whatever is just, whatever is pure, whatever is lovely, whatever is gracious, if there is any excellence, if there is anything worthy of praise, think about these things. — Philippians 4:8

Before I launch into my thoughts on keeping our eyes wide open, we need to go back to an episode of *Little House on the Prairie*. (If you weren't a viewer, think of any old western with plow horses.) The horses working in the field or hauling the family to town in the wagon often wore blinders. These little square leather pieces were meant to focus horses on the path and avoid distractions. It seems logical and safe, don't you think? There are days I think it would be helpful to have a pair so that I could focus on one task at a time instead of looking around, seeing a dozen things to do, and jumping from task to task.

Sometimes we are like those horses with blinders — we plow full speed ahead, focused on one thing. The problem, though, is when we struggle with a lack of peace, leading us to anxiety and worry. The thing we're laser focused on is usually adding to our struggle instead of leading us away from it. Being wide-eyed means we notice what's on the other side of those blinders.

There are a hundred things wrong with this world today. There is tragedy, violence, disaster, and evil in all corners of the globe. There is also sorrow, pain, sickness, financial struggle, relationship trouble, and plain ole worry settled into all the corners of our daily life. It's so easy to get caught with blinder vision and see only those things. Saint Paul in his letter to the Philippians encouraged them to look wider, and he even told them exactly what to focus on.

Today, I'm going to pull a Saint Paul and tell you exactly the same thing. You absolutely can see the yuck … there is a lot of it! But I'm going to encourage you to take off the blinders and look to the left and to the right. I'm going to ask you to look for the things that are good, just, noble, and lovely, the places God has touched with his goodness and peace. Now, I don't for one hot second want to diminish the reality of the hurt and confusion that may be sitting on your heart; I'm just asking you to notice all the other stuff God is showing you. Bad news always leads. Lies and negative spins on stuff seem more sparkly than a story about a four-year-old spending all his birthday money to buy cake mixes to make cupcakes for the firefighters and policemen in his neighborhood, which he sweetly delivered in his little red wagon. A story about deceit and violence will get more reads, likes, and comments than the article about NICU nurses who dressed preemies for Halloween.

It's a good idea to take down the blinders and see what you're missing. We have to ask hard questions and make tough choices, like turning off the news and cutting back or eliminating social media and other things that are eroding our peace and feeding our worry and anxiety. When I quit watching the news, I was afraid I'd be out of the loop. The funny thing is that I didn't really want to be in the loop in the first place. Another funny thing: The world didn't change when I stopped watching the circus — but I did.

We live in a world of great people doing great stuff. Do you see it? I was inspired by a generous, grateful act of Saint Gianna and her husband Pietro, one that went without notice to nearly everyone. At the birth of each of their children, they offered a sizable sum of money to the missions to pass their gratitude for God's generosity to others. What a beautiful idea! Giving generously in any way out of love is powerful. Sometimes the gesture is on a smaller scale, but it's no less powerful. I had a visit from a group of fifth-grade boys on Halloween night who brought me hot coffee, and I had a student who copied my favorite Scripture verse in perfect cursive with a glitter gel pen … beautiful!

I watched a sixth-grade brother visit his first-grade sister who forgot her lunch, delivering half of everything that was in his lunch pail. The sandwich was torn in half and half a bag of Doritos was poured onto the sandwich and wrapped in a paper towel. He split the apple in half with desk scissors and gave her one of his two Hershey Kisses. The whole exchange happened in silence behind the coat rack in my classroom. Words aren't needed to define that kind of love and humility. I still cry every time I remember that morning. If I hadn't been wide-eyed, I would have missed something beautiful.

If you're struggling, I'll ask you to look for the positive, the good, the lovely, and the excellent going on all around you. If you love someone who is struggling, I'll ask you to point it out and maybe even be the one who creates a little positive event in his or her life. A note or text and a flower or favorite snack delivered anonymously or personally with a hug and a prayer make a huge difference.

One more thought. When we're struggling, there is nothing that can pull us out of a slump faster than turning our focus to someone else. If I'm having a lousy day, seeing only my own yuck, doing a positive act for someone can snap me out of a funk faster than anything I can think of. A favorite movie of mine is

The Shack, and there's a particular line that just seems to bring peace and fit with the idea of having our eyes wide open. The line comes when God is speaking to Mack, and God says, "When all you see is your own pain, you lose sight of me."

To grow in joyful peace: As you seek and pray for peace, keep your eyes open and look for the positive things Saint Paul points us to. Don't forget to write them down as a reminder of his love.

St. Gianna Beretta Molla, pray for us!

The Next Step

I love the feeling I get when I finish a great spiritual book or wrap up an inspiring retreat or conference. There is a lift in my heart and a glow to my spirit. That is absolutely a gift from the Father, like a giant hug of encouragement and inspiration to continue my journey toward sainthood. In my mind, I have a spinning wheel of ideas, changes, additions, and adjustments I'd like to make to my holiness, and I often charge off in a blaze at a self-created pace. I have to be honest and admit that when I try to handle the process this way, one of two things usually happen: I either bite off way more than I can chew and end up feeling discouraged, or I get overwhelmed, busy, and don't actually make any fruitful adjustments at all, and the great book or retreat experience just withers like a plant I forgot to water.

I hope within the pages of this book you found encouragement, laughter, insight, and some nudges that fueled your desire to live joyfully in closer relationship with the Father. Now that you've finished this book, I'd like to offer some ideas about how to live the message. In the introduction I talked about that eggplant I took home from the farmers' market and watched spoil because it didn't come with a "what next" process. So if you'll stick with me just a wee bit longer, I'd like to lead you through a simple process so that the fruits of the saints, Scripture, and stories that spilled out in each chapter can be your guide to joyfully and fruitfully growing in your sainthood.

The first thing I would invite you to do is set this book in your prayer area for a bit and ask the Holy Spirit to prepare your heart for the work he'd like to do there. Invite him to show you the parts he really wants to "stick." After you've prayed a bit, open the book to the table of contents and pick a gift or a saint that touched your heart. If you're called to focus on one of the gifts, it might be one you see prominently in this season of your life, and you'd like to celebrate it, or perhaps it's a gift you struggle to embrace and find joy in. As you look back, you might find that it is a particular saint you are drawn to. Maybe your life shares similar struggles or situations. We were not created to live in isolation; we were meant for connection and relationship, and the saints powerfully stand at the ready for us to turn to for guidance, example, and mighty intercession. The lives of the saints are the mentorship we need to bridge the gap between worldview and God-view. The second thing I would invite you to do is jot down in your prayer journal a Scripture passage or two from the section of the book you were drawn back to and include them in your daily prayer, asking the Lord to reveal his truth and compassion in those particular words.

Christ is continuously inviting us to go out into the deep, and he leads us there a little bit at a time. He isn't going to drag us from ankle deep to the deepest depths in a flash. He meets us where we are and lovingly draws us closer, so don't be afraid to ask him the big questions. Father, what are you asking me to let go of? Father, how do you desire to make me more like your Son? Father, who/what are you inviting me to follow, and who/what are you inviting me to step away from? As he begins to guide us, he provides the grace to move forward, and the saints are our companions. Oftentimes the ways he invites us to shift and change are scary, but we're not alone, and he doesn't impose a deadline. It's good to remember that the definition of joy is being in the will of the Father, so any direction he leads us in is the right direction, and knowing we're trying to follow is a joyful realization.

Finally, don't be afraid to dig a little deeper. If you connected with one of the six saintly companions, learn more about them. Their lives are a treasure trove of wisdom, inspiration, and direction. The saints are "our people," so learn all you can about your new heavenly friend. If you were drawn to a particular gift, learn more about it. We are so blessed to have at our fingertips writings and teachings about so many things that can help us grow in holiness and joyfully travel the journey to heaven. If you aren't sure you have the time to dig deeper, one final challenge I'd offer is to take an honest look at how you spend your days and see if there might be minutes you can trade for doing something to bring glory to God. In the beginning, a saint, virtue, or Scripture study might not seem as entertaining or easy as binging your favorite shows on Netflix, but the time and effort will produce joy, and joy is a life-changing fruit of a relationship with our creator.

Please know of my prayers for each person who finds this book in his or her hands. I'll be praying that the Holy Spirit and the six saintly companions will bring you joy and lead you to live out the Father's plan for your life.

Acknowledgments

I offer complete and joyful thanks to the Holy Spirit for all the words that spilled out onto the pages of this book. The apostle Paul was supported, encouraged, and challenged by Barnabas, and I wonder what Paul's ministry would have been like without him. Knowing how important it is to have a Barnabas, I'd like to thank all those who are a Barnabas to me.

About the Author

Sheri is a passionate, joyful, coffee-loving daughter of God! She is a Catholic wife, mom, speaker, writer, grandma, and retired teacher. She's also a big fan of the Holy Spirit and spreading the love and joy of the Lord. The mission of her Catholic speaking and writing ministry is to spread the Gospel message in a practical, relatable, humorous way that invites, inspires, and challenges people to "see Christ" and "be Christ" in the world.

She uses her great sense of humor and her deep faith to help others discover the joy of being a child of God. Her roots are in Kansas, but her home is in Westphalia, Michigan. Sheri and her husband, Dave, have been married more than thirty years. She is the mother of three adult children and the grandmother of some completely adorable little humans! Sheri has a degree in secondary education from Emporia State University in Emporia, Kansas, and a master's degree in elementary education from Aquinas College in Grand Rapids, Michigan.

